Social Media Victimization

Social Media Victimization

Theories and Impacts of Cyberpunishment

Jessica Emami

LEXINGTON BOOKS
Lanham • Boulder • New York • London

Published by Lexington Books
An imprint of The Rowman & Littlefield Publishing Group, Inc.
4501 Forbes Boulevard, Suite 200, Lanham, Maryland 20706
www.rowman.com

86-90 Paul Street, London EC2A 4NE

British Library Cataloguing in Publication Information Available

Library of Congress Cataloging-in-Publication Data Is Available

ISBN: 978-1-7936-2964-7 (cloth)
ISBN: 978-1-7936-2965-4 (electronic)

Dedication

Dedicated with love to my spouse and my mother.

Contents

Foreword

Using social media to declare another person "persona non grata" is the contemporary form of the centuries-old practice of shunning. Though the practice of shunning negates and isolates the individual, the ubiquitous presence of social media can have a significant and profound impact on a person's life and livelihood beyond their immediate community. The communicative act of cancelling functionally serves to dehumanize and delegitimize the very existence of the "Other" such that the Other is not only Untermenschen (subhuman) but also does not even exist in the mind of the individual making the declaration of cancellation. Sadly, we have ample evidence throughout human existence of how such acts can lead to discrimination, repression, violence, and even genocide. Cancelling not only rejects the Other but also denies the Other the innate and pancultural human need for connection and acceptance by others; it negates the other as a viable human being: a person of worth, of being *somebody*.

A long-time colleague of mine refers to this state of being as social death, a place of alienation from others. The social and psychological effects of such relational isolation can be profound, resulting in severe anxiety, anger, psycho-emotional trauma, and even self and other-directed violent and destructive behavior. Alternatively, acknowledgment is the life-giving force that enables one to connect relationally with others and to be deemed worthy of existing as a meaningful being. While acknowledgment is a sustained openness to and expressed affirmation of others, cancellation is the antithesis of acknowledgment. Cancellation is the act of making another person "invisible."

But why do people cancel rather than acknowledge their neighbors? The same basic needs that we as humans have for affirmation and acknowledgment are the driving forces that motivate acts of denial. The need to believe that our existence matters and that we are somebody prompts us to deny others to be acknowledged by those from whom we seek affirmation. Two theoretical lenses that speak to this dynamic are Terror Management Theory (TMT) and Quest for Significance Theory (QST).

Briefly, TMT is based on the seminal work of Ernst Becker who claimed human consciousness of death gives rise to an existential terror of mortality. This fear of death is the basis for humankind's singular quest to know who they are, to be of primary value to human existence, to be of unquestionable meaning, and thus to "count" to others. Comparatively, QST proposes that the pursuit of personal significance is central to humankind's sense of meaning and purpose; it is a fundamental desire to be someone, to matter, and to have meaning. According to the authors of QST, being deemed worthy of being somebody, of being "significant" within a given society by other members of one's social and cultural group, is the essence that enables one to achieve a sentiment of significance.

Though distinct, both theories explain a basic human need to be significant, to be somebody to count for others. And, it is our need for acknowledgment that causes us to fear our mortal existence and which compels us to procure a sentiment of significance to buffer against our impending death. Do we truly exist absent acknowledgment from others? Our visceral anxiety about being alone in this world and spiritually separated from God drives our quest for acknowledgment from others to validate our existence and being as a self. Absent acknowledgment by others, we will fail to realize our quest for significance. Before we can realize self-love significance, we first must be acknowledged as existing and being worthy of being a self. In this way, acknowledgment is the critical communicative antecedent and linchpin in the human quest for meaning and significance to buffer against our existential reality. Dr. Emami uses these paradigms to effectively interrogate the phenomenon that she explores in this book, applying them insightfully and thoughtfully.

It was while attending a conference in Florida a couple of years ago that I first met Dr. Emami. During that time we struck up a conversation about our shared interest in social media, cancel culture, and potential social-psychological motivations to explain the phenomenon. I shared my ideas about how social psychology and communication research on motives for violent extremism might lend themselves to the phenomenon of cancel. We discussed the issue at length, including her desire to write this book. Her solid academic background, keen interest in the topic, and methodological approach to conducting her research substantiated her undertaking of this critically important project. The incidents that she critiques in this book and the theoretical lens that she employs shed important light on the phenomenon of cancel culture and the impact that such acts have on the individual target and society at large. The book is an important contribution to the body of work that investigates and seeks to explain the phenomenon of social media-based cancellation.

Randall G. Rogan, PhD
Wake Forest, NC

Acknowledgments

This is a book I have wanted to write since the early days of email and "America Online." As I marveled at the capabilities of the digital world and later cringed in horror at the conflicts exacerbated by internet technology, I began to wonder why, and how, humans are willing to demonstrate extraordinary cruelty to others online.

My acknowledgments for idea developments go to Rachel M. Hopp, Terri Lapinsky and Rachel M. Hopp. Academics who gave me tremendous support and insights include Randall G. Rogan, Corinne Blackmer, Matt Bakker, Janine DeWitt, R. Amy Elman, Hale Inanoglu, Virginia D'Antonio, Shannon Davis, Kathleen Lowery, and Sandra Hanson. I consulted with many about their experiences and specialized knowledge of cyberharassment and media theory, including Professor Daliah Saper of Saper Law, Chicago, IL, David L. Bernstein at the Jewish Institute for Liberal Values, Jacqueline Lavi Saper, Cathy Young, and Sarah Braasch.

My thanks go to the editors at Lexington Books for their interest in this book and their assistance in getting it from an idea to a book.

Introduction

The public has always strongly appreciated communication technology for its ability to bring people together. Media scholar and devotee Marshall McLuhan, for example, was watching the satellite simulcast of Neil Armstrong's moonwalk in 1969 when he felt that experiencing that historic event at the same time as millions of others scattered around the world made him a member of a "global village." Going forward, he stated, electronic media would cause fellow humans in distant places to be so greatly connected as to enable us to feel "primordial" sensations together.[1] McLuhan believed that electronic media had recaptured a sense of primordial tribal identity that had been lost due to modernity, stating, "We are back in acoustic space. We have begun again to structure the primordial feeling, the tribal emotions from which a few centuries of literacy divorced us." More importantly, he believed that electronic media had placed everyone together into a global tribe.

McLuhan's ideas were accurate in two regards: electronic communications technology fundamentally quickened the speed of life and shrank spaces and aroused intense primordial feelings around shared media experiences. These two properties would come not only to accelerate messaging to save lives but also to provide entertainment, and later on social media, to create chaos, cacophony, vexation, and destruction.

For most of the 20th century, the analog era, it was relatively easy for the public to feel optimistic about electronic media's potential for bringing people together and providing entertainment. These communications also necessitated the use of so much sophisticated and expensive equipment and expertise that only a handful of well-organized broadcasting companies could produce and deliver content. Media companies invested large sums in understanding and producing formats and content that could capture and sustain the public's attention and spent much money on in-house experts whose sole purpose was to entertain. A small number of powerful advertising companies streamlined the ways and means that broadcasters could fund their productions.

Although some parents and religious groups consistently expressed concern about the morality of particular content, the centralized control of production meant that when such concerns arose, the public knew exactly who produced it and where existing copies were located. Moreover, both the technology and the policy landscape and regulatory environment surrounding the technology were far less complex than it is today.

There was also great clarity about who produced and consumed content. Consumers were generally not the same social actors as producers, and given the technological structural complexity and consumers' economic limitations, they could not and did not expect to be.

Over time, however, advances in miniaturization, video compression, and the analog-to-digital transition of the late 20th century enabled a greater proportion of the general public to produce and transmit their own content. With the advent of digital platforms and the capability of consumers to upload their own messages and content, online media has become a veritable global jungle.

One effect of this jungle has been for people to use their ability to express themselves on social media as a platform to seek acknowledgment of their worldview, and to defend against those expressing views that threaten their worldview. In seeking to accomplish this venal task, everyone on social media escalates arguments, sparring on newsfeeds with others and pursuing the firing or humiliation of those with whom they disagree or whom they believe are immoral. This work addresses the ways these escalations begin and manifest in a cascade of punishing actions by users against one another.

In chapter 1, I describe the psychosocial reasoning behind why people become deeply entrenched in our online arguments the way they wouldn't in ordinary physical interaction. I introduce Dr. Randall Rogan's Quest for Acknowledgment Theory, which has as its underlying pillars both Terror Management Theory and Quest for Significance Theory.[2] Rogan's theory demonstrates that the quest for acknowledgment is a moral theory that is rooted in the same motivation that drives extreme behavior in radicalized terrorists. In the face-to-face interaction and in the digital world, the consequences are grave. I also use the political theory of consociationalism to explore the ways that current social media platforms that use text walls and pictures and videos, such as Twitter and Facebook, aggregate users in ways that prevents them from knowing their commonalities, and sets them up for polarization.

Chapter 2 traces the ways in which events that happen online become deeply connected and yet somewhat segregated from the physical world. I examine Jeffrey Lane's *The Digital Street* to analyze incidents that involve a stream of offline and online events that are interconnected but that leave those who don't know the "full story" wondering what is going on. I examine the various ways abuse and abusive content is created either online, then moving offline, or vice versa, illustrating that the physical and online world are interconnected but can also be disjointed due to the ability of social media to conceal contextual information.

In chapter 3 I examine how the use of a photo or video for context surrounding the story that goes viral can result in highly erroneous judgments about what we see. Using the story of the incident between some Catholic school students at an anti-abortion march who came into contact with Native Americans and African Americans at a separate march, I demonstrate how deceptive the use of photos and videos can be when making judgments about events posted. This chapter uses the ideas of Walter Benjamin,[3] Henri Cartier-Bresson,[4] and Barry Goldstein,[5] to show the curated and deceptive nature of photos and videos.

Chapter 4 uses Ervin Goffman's *Presentation of Self in Everyday Life*[6] and John Meyrowitz's *No Sense of Place*[7] to describe how social media has disrupted the concept of Erving Goffman's "frontstage" and "backstage" without disposing of their existence. Indeed, frontstage and backstage are discursive and meandering in the online environment and constantly juxtaposed with the physical world, with social media users attempting to manipulate the moving "backstage," the part of their inner world they expect their audiences never to see or know. I use the tragic story of Professor James Aune to review how an online fraudster was able to successfully deceive such an intelligent, intuitive person.

Chapter 5 is a study of how online environments enable "yellow" or deceptive journalism. Using James O'Keefe of the Veritas project as an example, I demonstrate how camera miniaturization and politicization enable people with no background in journalism to produce sensational and untruthful "news." This chapter also focuses on the ways in which the amateurization of news has contributed to an inability to discern fact from fiction.

The conclusion to this book explains how the internet and social media have brought people around the world into contact with one another, energized social movements, as well as created a treacherous atmosphere of conflict in which people pursue one another's punishment. I examine the technological shortcomings of online media platforms as well as the inhumane speed of information travel to emphasize that the technology itself is implicated in the current environment of ubiquitous conflict and the pursuit of punishing others online.

NOTES

1. McLuhan, M., Q. Fiore, and J. Agel. *The Medium Is the Massage: An Inventory of Effects* (San Francisco: HardWired, 1966/1996).

2. Dugas, Michelle, and Arie W. Kruglanski, "The Quest for Significance Model of Radicalization: Implications for the Management of Terrorist Detainees." *Behavioral Sciences & the Law* 32(3) (2014): 423–39. doi: 10.1002/bsl.2122.

3. Leslie, Esther. 2015. "Walter Benjamin and the Birth of Photography." In *On Photography*, edited and translated by Esther Leslie (London: Reaktion Books, 2015).

4. "Henri Cartier-Bresson and the Value of Photography." 2019. The Cambridge Student. January 30, 2019. https://www.tcs.cam.ac.uk/henri-cartier-bresson-and-the-value-of-photography/.

5. Goldstein, Barry M. 2007. "All Photos Lie: Images as Data." In *Visual Research Methods: Image, Society, and Representation*, edited by Gregory C. Stanczak. Thousand Oaks: SAGE Publications. http://www.library.yorku.ca/e/resolver/id/2331914.

6. Meyrowitz, J. *No Sense of Place: The Impact of Electronic Media on Social Behavior* (London: Oxford University Press, 1986).

7. Goffman, E. *The Presentation of Self in Everyday Life* (New York: Anchor Books/Doubleday, 1959/1999).

Chapter 1

This Is an Outrage!

THE FIRST MODERN CANCELLATION

On Valentine's Day 1989, a short time before the advent of the internet or social media, the first modern-time punishment decree took place against a well-known novelist, Salman Rushdie.[1] Ayatollah Khomeini, a cleric who had come to power and created a theocratic state in Iran in 1979, publicly condemned this famous writer to death for writing a satire about the Prophet Mohammed. Using a religious decree, or *fatwa*, Khomeini offered a reward of US$1,000,000 to anyone who killed Rushdie on sight.[2] Rushdie stated he found out about the *fatwa* after being contacted by a reporter who asked him how it feels to know that his "old life is over and a new, darker existence was about to begin." He told the reporter it did not feel very good but thought to himself that he was a dead man.[3]

This decree sent Rushdie into hiding, condemned to "social death"—a condition in which Rushdie could not be acknowledged or seen publicly for fear of death, resulting in alienation, isolation, and depression—unable to be seen in public, and losing touch with core members of his social groups: colleagues, family, friends, and others.[4,5] The isolation profoundly affected his ability to freely express his social self and social identities. Had he been in Iran, the *fatwa* may well have meant physical death. For nine years, even as the next Iranian leader renewed the *fatwa*, Rushdie moved from place to place under the protection of the British Government. In short, his life was permanently negatively altered.[6]

Others involved in the production of his book have also been targeted. In 1991, Japanese translator Hitoshi Igarashi was murdered by stabbing, and Italian translator Ettore Capriolo survived stabbing. Norwegian publisher William Nygaard was shot thrice in 1993, and Turkish translator and world-renowned satirist Aziz Nesin's hotel room was set on fire in 1993, killing 37 people. In 2015, writer and South African Muslim novelist Zaynap P. Dala was beaten savagely and placed in a mental institution for expressing admiration for Rushdie.[7,8] Sadly, the *fatwa* remains in force today.[9,10]

MODERN DAY ONLINE SOCIAL DEATH DECREES

These days, motivated by moral outrage and enabled by the internet-worked structure of social media platforms, lesions of internet users act in synchrony to punish targets they do not know in person and whose only claim to fame may be that they have been targeted for punishment on the internet or on social media. The tactics and degrees of punishment vary, but like Ayatollah Khomeini, social media users target others out of a view that their targets have morally transgressed in some way. In response, they issue personal *fatwas* in concert with other social media users, with the collective conviction to punish their targets, and causing lasting and profound damage.

VARIETIES OF CYBERPUNISHMENT

Before venturing far into cyber misbehavior, it is useful to examine the basic categories of cyber misbehavior in federal law. The US Department of Justice has five basic groups of internet cyber misbehavior that overlap and carry legal consequences: cyberbullying, cyber threats, cyberstalking, cyber harassment, and cyber extortion.[11]

Cyberbullying is defined as "unwanted, aggressive behavior performed digitally on websites, social media, chatrooms, cell phones and computers."[12] Cyber threats consist of "threats to harm someone, communicated digitally."[13] These threats are generally intended to make victims feel targeted and intimidated. Spreading rumors are a form of cyber threat. Cyberstalking includes repeatedly engaging in intrusive, unwanted communications with targets over cell phones or computers. Victims of cyberstalking generally fear serious injury and can become severely and emotionally distressed.

Cyber harassment includes threatening or harassing through emails or posts, but also swatting and doxing. Swatting is defined as "causing, special weapons and tactics (swat) officers or emergency responders to be dispatched to the victims address and places the victim and law enforcement at great risk."[14] Doxing is defined as broadcasting personally identifiable information, such as telephone numbers and home addresses, over the internet. It is used to incite others to physically confront targets, while giving the doxers distance and plausible deniability.[15,16]

Cyber extortion is defined as soliciting something of value through "actual or threatened force, violence or fear."[17] These include sextortion or "demanding a person provide the perpetrator with sexual images or other things of value, schemes in which perpetrators use flattery or friendship to gain the victims confidence to obtain nude photos and subsequently blackmail the victims for money."[18] The range of misbehavior encompasses vast and overlapping system of consequences for both perpetrator and victim. For victims, the consequences can range from feeling intimidated, anxious, or in fear for their life, to mortal fear and in some egregious cases, death by homicide or suicide.

The law is clear that repeatedly targeting someone even with only words has legal implications. But this has not stopped many people from using the internet against other individuals to assert their own moral beliefs or enforce social norms. Digital sociologists and legal scholars have found that behaviors such as shaming and doxing serve the purpose of social control and norm enforcement. Digital sociologist danah boyd states that, in addition to shining a spotlight on people for being virtuous or heroic, "people are made visible to use them as an example . . . or to set an example. People are outed to reveal hypocrisy and their practices are made visible to shame them."[19] In most of the population, the immediate result of this ostracism is severe pain and distress.[20]

Keeping in mind the sociological context of norm enforcement, that is, that of battling racism, homophobia, or other types of prejudice using digital platforms, others believe that cyberpunishment has a useful and constructive purpose. In the context of racism, for example, sociologist Apryl Williams argues that denigrating memes about those perceived to be racist busybodies is justified.[21] She views the memes as a "cultural critique of White surveillance and White racial dominance" and believes they serve to neutralize White dominance by silencing the targets. The memes, in her opinion, are an essential form of "agency in the struggle for racial equity."[22]

The objective of this chapter is to explore how the targets' behavior comes to be perceived as unacceptable, how coordinated online actions can often escalate and lead to punishments that far outweigh the actual or perceived transgressions, and how technology mediates this "cyberpunishment." I attempt to answer the following questions: how and why do some people go out of their way to broadcast controversial views to the general public knowing the possible ramifications? How and why do groups of unrelated people on social media exert such great social power to punish? What does this punishment entail? Does the punishment ultimately right moral wrongs? And how does social media mediate this process of identification and targeting?

The internet has surely brought many advantages to modern society. But this chapter and book focus on the negative ramifications of punishing others online for something they have said or done that has been perceived as a moral wrong. Some of the targets do indeed behave abhorrently, and many times the causes—such as racism, sexism, workers' rights, and body pride—are just. But all too often the targets are individuals with little agency who are condemned for years or a lifetime because of a single action or brief exchange that creates an appearance of immorality. Using a variety of sociological, communications, psychological, and political theories, I attempt to explain this online digital pillory. Lastly, I briefly explore some ideas for policy tools to mitigate social media targeting.

SOCIAL DEATH DECREES VARY, BUT SOME DO KILL

Although online groups do not often call for their targets' physical deaths, the swiftness and force of their virtual condemnation can be so severe that, once spawned, the invective rarely dies. For example, it is not uncommon for online posts to call for targets to be immediately fired, that is, to lose their livelihoods.[23,24,25] Employers rarely resist such pressure, lest they too become targets. Indeed, the initial blow against the targets can be so severe that they and their families may lose their income, their housing, their health benefits, and most importantly their professional reputation, within a matter of days or hours. They may also lose their partners or spouses from the pressures of the decrees.

The stress of being alienated and socially dead often leads to physical stress and disintegration.[26,27,28] The norm-enforcing groups foment a "death of the soul"[29] to maintain dominance over their targets.[30] The impacts on the target can be devastating. A target can be repeatedly ridiculed, or outed, to one new employer after another, often becoming permanently unemployable. Some targets become depressed and attempt suicide—and even complete suicide.[31]

MORAL OUTRAGE: THE KEY TO INTERNET PUNISHMENTS

Although there are large differences between the Rushdie case and today's social media targets of punishment, there are also similarities to the Rushdie case. First, like the mobs following the Ayatollah's instructions around the globe, social media users act in synchrony to issue virtual *fatwas* against others they have deemed to be immoral. The moral outrage, the sense of entitlement to vigilante action, and the global reach of the internet are like the Rushdie case.

Virtual *fatwas* on social media usually revolve around specific moral—and sometimes political—causes or beliefs. For example, users may target someone whom they believe is fascist, racist, misogynist, transphobic, homophobic, and others. The degree of conviction in the correctness of their position and the harshness of the invective they hurl at their targets often rise to an internet frenzy that evokes the sense of an existential moral crisis. Participants turn to social media to sanction people whose attitudes, speech, actions, or demeanor they deem morally repugnant.

Rushdie's case arose through the moral outrage of a ruthless theocratic leader with legitimate state power. Moreover, both Rushdie and Khomeini were already known to the world through the mainstream media prior to the *fatwa*, enabling Rushdie to quickly be spotted and punished if he dared to appear in public. Social media's networked structure today simulates the traditional media of the 1980s but acts more quickly and so enables people who are not famous to quickly become known on a global scale. The various algorithms of the platforms promote the spread of the scandalous story as increasing numbers of people seek out or react to the story.

Although social media actors do not act under a state authority as Ayatollah Khomeini did, the way technology promotes and aggregates social media finger-pointers with one another—by chance or not—enables them to react with strong moral conviction and vehemently pursue the punishment of the target. These properties of aggregation, speed, and moral conviction enable and mimic the Rushdie *fatwa* issuance. Once issued, the target's life, livelihood, health, and sanity can be damaged temporarily or permanently.

MOTIVATING FACTORS

What motivates such high-stakes moralizing of social values common to an online interest group? What do they seek by judging and targeting the morality of others? What compels targets to publicly declare their moral views on a platform that any stranger or one's mother or boss could see? Why do conflicting views on social media escalate so frequently and in ways that do not usually occur in the physical world?

One explanation of the viciousness of some online actors' "callouts" of others on social media is the theory of deviance by sociologist Emil Durkheim.[32] He believed that pointing out deviance serves the valuable purpose of reinforcing the social solidarity of the main social group. The presumed lack of values of the *deviant* would stand out as distinct from the group itself. Casting out a specific deviant from the main group signals to everyone in the group what values the group members must adhere to in order to remain a member.[33] This classic theory explains much of the way society's treatment of deviance functions on- or offline.

But this theory does not explain the reasons people resort to social media to announce their political and moral views knowing full well that some others—sometimes many others—could object to their views and target them. Nor does Durkheim's theory of deviance explain why online moral battles with people we don't even know personally often escalate. There is a disconnect between the randomness of encounters on the internet or social media and the personal offense many people take when they encounter others they vehemently disagree with.

THE QUEST FOR SIGNIFICANCE AND ACKNOWLEDGMENT

A better explanation for motivations behind the pitched online battles lies in the theories of communication and psychology that have recently developed from studies of those radicalized in terrorist circles. Although it may feel outlandish to use theories of radicalization to understand social media wars, the impetus of social media users to initiate, perpetuate, and engage in escalating and often ugly social conflict has elements and processes in common with the radicalization of terrorists. These include the Quest for Significance Theory (QST),[34] Terror Management Theory (TMT),[35,36] and a theory that combines the two, Randall G. Rogan's theory of the quest for acknowledgment.[37,38]

The impetus for committing malign activity in radicalized terrorist networks and groups has been explained by the Quest for Significance Theory (QST) developed by Ernest Becker[39] and Arie Kruglanski et al.[40] In QST, individuals have the fundamental desire to matter, to feel significant and worthy of self-respect.[41] Every human being must be validated by others to buffer existential anxiety associated with threats to their worldview.[42] In Ernest Becker's *The Birth and Death of Meaning*,[43] he states that human beings initially obtain their sense of security and being at one with the world from the physically nurturing bosom of their parents. As children grow older, they earn and cultivate cultural and symbolic praise from their parents and later attempt to maintain this fragile sense of security by themselves.[44]

Becker further notes that by affirming their worldview, expressing it, and obtaining approval and reinforcement from our peer groups and other social networks, we reinforce our sense of security and affirm our own cultural worldview.[45] Kruglanski et al.[46] and Rogan[47] also emphasize that the confirmation of our worldview is derived from our social groups. Based on Rousseau's concept of self-love or *amour propre*, the confirmation of our worldview and cultural identity depends on positive feedback and recognition by others. In self-love, the person is motivated by wanting to "count," to "matter."[48] By contrast, those ostracized or in solitary confinement suffer precisely because they are prevented from "counting" by other humans.

TERROR MANAGEMENT THEORY (TMT)

Becker[49] stated that human beings are one of the only species to consciously realize and constantly and mentally ward off mortality. This awareness in Becker's view is the source of our constant strive to seek meaning for our lives, in other words, to become immortal. Where other animals live in the present and act by instinct, humans ruminate about their mortality because they have awareness of it. Our cultural framework and its affirmation are tied up with our sense of security and our desire to ward off mortality. In short, humans desire to feel significant to ward off anxieties about their own mortality. From a very early age, Becker states that the conscious knowledge of our mortality renders our question of significance and security a thoroughly existential matter.

Pursuing and defending our sense of security, our worldview is framed by our learned cultural values, which came from our parents. Defense of our worldview is therefore a matter of life and death. Our values-based battles and our quest to be acknowledged positively by others are often waged because we wish to avert our own death.

Combining elements of TMT[50] and QST,[51] Communications scholar Randall G. Rogan posits that underlying both TMT and QST is the singular motivation of craving significance, but more crucially, craving *acknowledgment*, something QST and TMT scholars have not focused on adequately.[52] Feedback by others, in Rogan's view, is a key element of the quest for significance and immortality. Most importantly, Rogan stipulates that the key motive for turning to others for feedback and acknowledgment is their bestowal of significance.

Thus, in the age of the internet, human beings turn to social media groups not only to spread their own beliefs and ideas before they die but also to seek acknowledgment and affirmation in the here and now from members of their own affinity groups. Acknowledgment, then, is the underlying motivation for all processes that reinforce our sense of personal dignity and incentivizes people on social media to place posts, elicit responses from others, and respond to others in kind. Moreover, when members of online social groups fall into conflict with others, they frequently express *animus* and engage in escalating social conflict, often posting more frequently in response to opposition, humiliation, and invective. The conflicting views frequently spiral into a chain of mutual punishment justified by our desire to defend against the annihilation of our worldview and thereby ourselves.

Every social actor seeks deep personal meaning in their relationships, including online relationships. Online social actors therefore join affinity groups to feed their yearning to matter in an existential sense. This same impetus motivates people to press ahead urgently in search of ways to spread their values and ideals to the world within their lifetime, to leave a legacy. This mortality salience explains the fame-seeking behaviors of people who post attention-seeking or fame-seeking material, or exhibit "preachy" behavior in their religious, ethical, or political points of view.

It is thus the desire to be acknowledged that both brings us closer together, embroils us in an escalating social media battle, or entices us to post controversial messages knowing full well there may be consequences. We wish for *our* worldview to be acknowledged and affirmed, in order for us to feel more secure in the world, to cement our place in society, and to find followers, fans, and peers who acknowledge us.

EVERYBODY ONLINE WANTS TO BE A HERO

One of the ways we ward off mortality in Rogan and Becker's view is by being a hero. Many heroes and most superheroes, after all, are immortal. Becker, and many other philosophers and authors such as Abraham Maslow, Sigmund Freud, and William James, believes that humans not only engage in a perpetual quest for security and meaning but also express this impetus by acting heroically.[53] In Becker's view, we all want to be heroes and to save the day in order to ensure our personal sense of security and self-esteem. Becker states, "not only the popular mind knew, but philosophers of all ages, in our culture, especially Emerson and Nietzsche. . . . That we like to be reminded that our central calling or main task on this planet is heroic."[54] One way heroism frequently manifests is by posting toward a cause we believe can save humanity, the earth, or some other major existential cause. Others post fame-seeking posts that encourage others to give a positive or negative acknowledgment, and by arguing with and recruiting supporters when faced with a user who expresses conflicting views. Social media provides the platform upon which to effect the desired goal of satisfying one's quest for significance, one's gaining of self-esteem through random members of the online community who substitute as our parents and our family members and networks.

In seeking to be an immortal hero, Becker believes we all often grapple with the same basic and existential questions but have clashing answers.[55] Social media users often shout their viewpoints from their rooftops and add them onto their social media news walls or Twitter feeds. They explain the values that help them feel physically secure and spiritually at one with the world, realizing their potential for self-actualization, and heroism, but also creating potential conflicts.

THE MEDIA, A MATERIAL CULTURE HERO SYSTEM

Human beings' quest for immortality, as we have seen, is a spiritual quest. But according to Becker, spiritual self-actualization or "at-oneness" in the modern era has necessarily shifted from religion to an empty science of the material world, what he terms the "material culture hero systems." These include finding heroism in loyalty to a corporation, to debauchery and promiscuity, to a branch of science, a political party, a nation, or even a global cause.[56]

Unfortunately, this reliance on fragile material systems as the source for self-actualization has created a spiritual crisis for the many secular working and poor classes having lost their faith in traditional religion and hero systems and do not have access to the luxuries of material culture.[57]

One of the greatest sources of spirituality in the modern era has come from media devotees and corporate gurus who spiritualize "miraculous" new technologies, including the media. For example, when Hernan Cortes disembarked from his ship in 1518 onto what is now Mexico, native Aztecs who saw him atop his horse in armor believed he was a god because they had never seen horses, white men, or armor.[58] In the case of electronic media, the science of how they work is opaque to most users and audiences, but its effects are immediate, visible, and powerful. Marconi and Alexander Graham Bell's first transmissions awed the entire world and continue to do so today in the history books.

Alex F. Osborne, the man who coined the term "brainstorming" in his book *Your Creative Power: How to Use Imagination*, viewed creativity as the factor that distinguishes humans from the animal kingdom and endows them with Becker's heroic qualities.[59] He believed that using creativity and brainstorming to unlock the power of innovation and new technology production made humans the navigators of their own unlimited destinies.

The television and the internet, too, have been idolized in quasi-spiritual terms. Many media devotees and scholars, and countless ordinary people, often attribute spiritual qualities to new electronic media when they first appear on the scene. In his *The Medium Is the Massage*, Marshall McLuhan gleefully praised the electronic media as a new spiritual frontier.[60] After the satellite simulcast of the US moon landing in 1967, McLuhan declared that a technological "global village" had just been created because millions of people watched the moon landing simultaneously. Evoking nirvana, he exclaimed, as if in a state of ecstasy, "ours is a brand new world of all-at-onceness, time has ceased and space has vanished."[61]

Forty years later, when the internet was launched to a smallish audience, it too evoked a sense of wonder, hope, and nirvana. The awe of a world in which every single individual in the world (with a computer) could transmit and receive messages from anyone else, anywhere else in the world, was initially unfathomable. Social media, and media more generally, gave hope to some that the sense of being at one with the world, that of bringing people together in a spirit of world peace and connection, could restore human spirituality and self-actualization. By the time web 1.0 appeared, the visual aspects of websites and web surfing and the development of the information superhighway had awed and amazed legions and branded a cadre of technology leaders such as Steve Jobs, Marc Andreessen, and Bill Gates as superheroes.

After social media such as MySpace and Facebook emerged, their initial impetus was to connect people in the spirit of camaraderie and enable them to express themselves to others on their network. People joined these fora with relish and glee, oblivious to the potential for social conflict. Soon, pent-up generations of traditional media users realize that they too could have a platform. They too mattered, they too could analyze, report, and pontificate. They too could be heroes and heroines.

As users channeled their innate desire to be acknowledged into their social media posts, they encountered friendship and connections, but also brutality and hatred from those whose cultural worldviews were dramatically opposed to theirs. Once others posted opinions that went against their fundamental moral beliefs, they were existentially threatened and felt the need to respond in order to suppress their own mortality and uphold their own worldview. They responded in kind with equal pushback and vehemence to ward off threats to their fundamental worldview.

On social media, literally anyone may see our posts, not just those who have similar viewpoints to ours. Social media is the space where random people from vastly different backgrounds and cultures interact around a post or work together in an online community based on one or just a few causes of action, without deeper knowledge of one another's personalities, traits, or values. We often do not know with whom we are dealing online, despite dealing extensively with many.

Affirming what Becker had stated in *The Birth and Death of Meaning*,[62] the most unpredictable area of social life, particularly on social media, was "the people." Becker believed life was chaotic because each person, seeking immortality, was executing their own heroics without necessarily knowing what motivated other people. People, after all, can have violent temper tantrums or other unpredictable behaviors. Thus, the pattern of interactions and physical and online worlds could become a play in which each person, bound by their quest for significance, their need to enact their cultural worldview, and to be their culture's hero, would impose their worldview upon others.

Soon, instead of being acknowledged and supported, they would be shunned, attacked, subdued, and humiliated online. The same impetus that created fame-seeking and acknowledgment compelled them to return a response, to correct the record, and to defend against existential threats to their worldview and their immortality.[63] This fueled online conflict, sometimes resulting in someone getting targeted in the physical world by a gathering storm of social media norm-enforcing opponents. The virtual *fatwa* was born.

SOCIAL MEDIA MAKES DIGITAL "*FATWAS*" MORE PROBABLE THAN IN THE PHYSICAL WORLD

We have seen that conflict can arise in the physical world and on social media. But is there something particular to the internet and social media that worsens social conflict and "digital *fatwas*"? Some scholars believe the impersonal nature of the news feed, the false sense of personal anonymity, and the speed and scope of the information flow can make conflicts online worse in scope and degree than in the physical world.[64] Notably, it is extremely difficult for current generations of social media to gain much contextual information about users in opposition groups. In the physical world, a more nuanced, restrained interaction ensues because by seeing people in person we can gain a better idea of what we may have in common with them. Online, however, the lack of physical cues and contextual information enables us to stereotype and mischaracterize those who have opposing views.

THE EMERGENCE OF "SMART MOBS"

First, the vast, internetworked structure of social media has enabled large numbers of unrelated people to coalesce around common singular interests or viewpoints and to act seemingly instantaneously in a coordinated way. This phenomenon was explained 21 years ago by the scholar of technology and society Howard Rheingold.[65] He noted that the enormous power of social movements in recent years has sprung from the combination of three technologies: mobile computing, communication networks, and information networks.

In the late 1980s, after the establishment of mobile phones that connected via cellular networks, users still did not have access to larger information pools such as location data and internet search engines. Those technologies did not come about until the 1990s. Those two capabilities brought about a sea change in the power of these groups and the speed with which they could connect and react. Platforms such as Facebook and Twitter, and for a time, Google+, connected people to one another and to sources of information. Rheingold called them "smart mobs" because they used technology to find one another based on their moral and ideological beliefs, to connect with one another, and more importantly to deploy concerted real-time action.

Rheingold was very distinctive in his use of the word *mob* and defined "smart mobs" as "mobile *ad hoc* social networks" made possible by computation, location, and communication.[66] Rheingold's "smart mobs" could act around one objective even if the people on the network did not know one another.[67] They gained a new, heretofore unprecedented social power, acting with both neighbors and people living a hemisphere away, and with the capacity to do just as much evil as good.

For example, Rheingold credited the mobile technological trifecta of mobile computation, location tracing, and access to large pools of information as the cause of the massive, late 1990s, anti-globalization movement that memorably challenged the World Trade Organization in Seattle in 1999.[68] In November of that year, members of labor, anti-globalization, and anarchist groups partnered with others to protest globalization's toll on the world. This was one of the first social actions to be organized using a combination of internet and text messaging.

About 40,000 participants comprised of a loose federation of social activist groups came together to protest for living wages, human rights, an end to human trafficking, and more. The AFL/CIO, the largest labor federation in the United States, organized a coordinated march of about 25,000 workers for labor rights. Protesters were able to livestream and coordinate their activities digitally using their mobile phones.[69] Rheingold also presciently noted that the internet can be used for bad acts as well. Writing 20 years ago, he wrote that it was too soon to predict whether the acquisition of a ubiquitous network would deliver convenience "faster than it erodes sanity and civility."[70] In Seattle in 1999, for example, some of the demonstrators chose violent tactics while using their cellphones to evade police and attacked and destroyed millions of dollars of property. Judging by the evolution of the information society since his writing, sanity and civility are increasingly lost to convenience.

Today, social media platforms such as Facebook and Twitter offer effective tools not only to organize billions of users into specific affinity groups with vast global reach, but these tools are often used to enact mob textual and verbal violence against others online. It is achieved when each user signals through the information they provide about themselves, photos and buttons on their profiles, their favorite brands, the groups they belong to, the philosophers and politicians they favor, animals they love, art they enjoy, political figures they admire, advocacy networks they belong to, hobbies they practice, entertainers they watch, sports they play or spectate, movies and music they consume, and newspapers and blogs they read. Activists concerned with hot button issues can instantaneously find public or private groups to interact with others who have the same opinions or concerns.

Users can also instantaneously circulate negative campaigning messages about their targets. The video platform service, YouTube, has billions of users and supports billions of easily searchable videos uploaded by anyone, anywhere, just about anything. Any activist can capture and upload an embarrassing video onto YouTube, and once uploaded, the video can be spawned elsewhere simultaneously even if the original post is taken down.[71,72] Other platforms also exist. For example, TikTok promotes stories that are liked or watched from beginning to end, or likes, so mobs who do these actions help embarrassing stories go viral. Facebook promotes posts that are commented on frequently, or liked in large numbers.

Users in these groups are not necessarily part of a social movement, but they are definitively looking to act around a specific viewpoint as online norm declarers and many times, norm enforcers. Norm-enforcing user groups frequently veer off into becoming online morality "police," vilifying, pillorying, and casting their targets out of public life.[73,74,75]

SOCIAL MEDIA AGGREGATE AROUND CAUSES AND INTERESTS, NOT PEOPLE

Taking a page from the political science playbook, if we view social media ecosystems as a political system, we can use the theory of *consociationalism*, a term coined by Anders Lijphart[76] with reference to political cleavages across political parties. In consociationalism, risks of deep social cleavages are mitigated when members of one party have overlapping commonalities with the opposing parties.

For example, if one political party contains only rich white men and the other poor minority workers, political conflict is likely to be quite high, leading to instability. On social media platforms, when a diverse set of strangers coalesce around a cause or an ideology, there is still a lack of contextual information about one another. Possible commonalities across ideological divides become impossible to know.[77] On social media, the lack of knowledge about cross-cutting interests across ideological cleavages makes the network groups unnecessarily rigid and severely divided. There is no mechanism for forming deeper relationships that provide the equivalent to face-to-face understanding. By contrast, a more nuanced restraint and resolution of normative differences in the physical world occurs because of the phenomenon called consociationalism.

THE INTERNET AND SOCIAL MEDIA ARE FOREVER

On the internet, due to crawling bots that capture social media content, as well as linking or copying content from site to site, attempts to quash embarrassing or controversial posts are futile because they pop up elsewhere. At times, such defensive efforts can even compound the problem as specific searching can increase the visibility of the posts. Removing an internet post is not unlike Hercules contesting the hydra with nine heads. Each time one head was chopped off, multiple heads grew back. Each time one site is shut down, scores more appear. The discursive and networked structure of the internet is such that no sensational story will truly completely disappear. This ensures that stories about targets replicate and remain on the internet perpetually, at the ready to be revealed by search engines. George Washington University Professor of Law Daniel Solove describes the permanence of the targeted as being "eternally preserved in electrons . . . forever in the digital doghouse. . . ."[78]

TARGETED, IDENTIFIED, MEMED

One instrument online norm enforcers use to shame and ostracize is the meme, a video, or photo spread on social media that represents an event or idea about a person that is passed on from one person to another. Many memes used by norm enforcement groups highlight specific people to identify and shame them. In 2005, for example, a woman in South Korea was walking her dog when the dog defecated on the ground. She refused to pick up the dog's poop and was captured on video. The "dog poop girl" meme was born and circulated so widely that she quit her university and turned to a career of writing media editorials about privacy and online shaming.[79]

The persistence of these denigrating memes on the internet and the reemergence of the public pillory amount not only to a culture in which "anonymous" online players can dehumanize whomever they wish to target but also signals the emergence of a perpetual, unconstrained, surveillance machine that silences everyone. The social and ethical repercussions of the phenomenon deserve serious scrutiny to prevent disintegration and unraveling of civil society.

THE SOCIAL MEDIA PANOPTICON: THE INTERNET SEES ALL

The emerging virtual surveillance machine of online communities and movements guard against "moral" incursions that undermine the "moral authority" authority of online political groups. These are are reminiscent of Jeremy Bentham's Panopticon, an all-seeing mechanism in prisons.[80] Bentham, an 18th-century architect, designed a mechanism for prisons that would enable administrators to exert institutional control over the prisoners through overwhelming surveillance and *threat* of surveillance. With its circular design, the guards had a view of each cell across the entire prison. In *Discipline and Punish*, philosopher Michel Foucault highlighted the self-administered discipline created within the prisoners' minds as a result of this all-encompassing surveillance. The panopticon produced self-discipline in the prisons because inmates did not know *if* they were being watched but also knew that they *could* be watched at any time.[81] The panopticon's ability to surveil subjects exerted pressure on them before any actions were taken against them, thus having effective "corrective" value at little cost.[82]

Today, digital technology has enabled masses to similarly act as both self-appointed prison administrators and targets of this all-encompassing digital disciplinary system. What norm enforcement groups fail to recognize is that they are participating in a disciplinary system that can make targets of anyone, including themselves, and benefits only the producers of the technology and the states that weakly govern them.[83] Today the internet is the new panopticon, a tool of "political technology"[84] that exercises both positive and negative power upon all its users. We never know who is recording our public interactions and where on the internet the videos may end up. Once uploaded to social media, its use as a tool of exposure and punishment is unrivaled in its ubiquity and ferocity.

Memes abound on digital media, and the derogatory memes often arise as a punishment for the target's antisocial behavior. But the core of cyberpunishment is often more complex than it seems. Some of the most egregious cases of cyberpunishment involve contested issues of race, religion, and core political beliefs. Although the norm enforcers are by no means a monolith, they do fall across specific sides of the sociopolitical divide, and often a battle of moral values plays out on both sides in cases against specific people.

In the United States, for example, many memes are circulated to shame and counter White people who have policed the activities of Black people. Memes such as these include "Pool Patrol Paula"[85] and "BBQ Becky."[86] All too often these cases deserve to be addressed, and there can be no question that society still has much to do to address racial bias. But in some instances, the incidents are on the scale of neighborhood *kerfuffels* that could have been resolved more satisfactorily for those directly involved with a handshake, counseling, or at most, small claims court. Such disputes would never be elevated to the level of a national story in normal circumstances. Nor do the punishments inflicted fit the sins. But powered by social media technology, the memes are broadcast with no opportunity for nuance or due process. The norm-enforcing groups act in synchrony, often creating sensations from everyday conflicts to connect to a larger grievance.

POSSIBLE SOLUTIONS TO MITIGATE NORM ENFORCEMENT GROUP TARGETING

Undoubtedly, the aggregating and targeting power of the internet and social media means that, barring major legal and technological reforms, people will continue to easily identify and target others online. As online viciousness becomes increasingly normalized, the echo chamber that relies on blaming, framing, and hunting down will also continue. George Washington University Law Professor Daniel Solove[87] cautioned on the extreme nature of norm enforcers on the internet, suggesting that the legal system must act to curb these excesses against even the worst offenders. Solove raises the point that norms enforced on social media and viral memes have a permanence that norm enforcement offline does not. He also addresses the disproportionality of the "crime" from the "punishment."

Some solutions that Solove proposes are the cautious expansion of laws governing defamation and invasion of privacy. Solove believes that a middle-way approach, one that stands between a *laissez faire* policy with the online world or an authoritarian approach that promotes internet censorship, is to use civil law, that is, lawsuits between private individuals. Torts governing defamation about a person online and invasion of privacy lawsuits are one possible measure to curb the excesses of online norm enforcement.

Relying solely on the development of a new system of normative behavior through private litigation, however, will take years and is not likely to be enough to close the rifts that are forming in society. It certainly will not be a practical remedy for unfairly targeted individuals. Who would they sue among the myriad actors in the norm enforcement groups? Where would they find the resources to pursue major corporations?

It will be up to our legislators, policy makers, corporations, and thought leaders to find a balance between freedom of expression and destroying lives and communities. What remains clear is that the phenomenon of public norm enforcement, online groups acting as judge, jury, and executioners will not end unless we act concertedly as a society to place limits on such activity.

During the darkest days of the Salman Rushdie affair, a cadre of 1,000 brave writers who were members of PEN International Network stood by

Rushdie to protect free expression.[88] But for years, the international community hedged in standing up for Rushdie in the effort to balance freedom of expression with freedom of religion.[89] As a result of their inaction, the Islamic Republic of Iran persisted, raising an additional $600,000 in 2016 for the Rushdie *fatwa*.[90] As we approach the 33rd year of this sordid *fatwa*, the international community now realizes the importance of standing up for principles of free expression and civic engagement[91] and the dire risks of unfettered mob justice. We the public must stand for these principles too, not only for public figures such as Rushdie but also for the least among us.

NOTES

1. Lin, Kimberly, "Salman Rushdie and the Iranian Fatwa," *Historic Mysteries*. September 2018. Accessed June 4, 2021. https://www.historicmysteries.com/salman-rushdie-fatwa/.
2. Rushdie, Salman, *Joseph Anton: A Memoir,* 1st edition (New York: Random House, 2012).
3. Rushdie, *Joseph Anton.*
4. Williams, Kipling D., "Ostracism: The Kiss of Social Death," *Social and Personality Psychology Compass* 1 (2007): 236–247.
5. Rogan, Randall G., "Acknowledgment as a Primary Motive for Violent Extremism," unpublished manuscript, Wake Forest, NC, 2018.
6. Rushdie, *Joseph Anton.*
7. PEN America, "PEN Outraged by Confinement of South African Writer Who Expressed Admiration for Rushdie," *PEN America,* April 2015. Accessed December 25, 2021. https://pen.org/pen-outraged-by-confinement-of-south-african-writer-who-expressed-admiration-for-rushdie/.
8. Smith, David, "South African Author ZP Dala Allegedly Coerced into Mental Hospital," *The Guardian,* April 2015. Accessed December 25, 2021. https://www.theguardian.com/world/2015/apr/12/south-african-muslim-author-z-p-dala-allegedly-coerced-mental-hospital.
9. Lin, "Salman Rushdie and the Iranian Fatwa."
10. On August 12, 2022, as this book was going to press, 33 years after Ayatollah Khomeini's *fatwa* was issued, Rushdie, now 75, was stabbed by an assailant while waiting to be introduced for a speech at the Chautauqua Institution in New York. He was permanently blinded in one eye and will have significant disability as a result of the stabbing.
11. Blanch, Joey L., and Wesley L. Hsu, "An Introduction to Violent Crime on the Internet," *United States Attorneys' Bulletin* 64, no. 3 (2016): 2–12.
12. Blanch and Hsu, "An Introduction to Violent Crime on the Internet."
13. Blanch and Hsu, "An Introduction to Violent Crime on the Internet," 3.
14. Blanch and Hsu, "An Introduction to Violent Crime on the Internet," 5.

15. Samuels, Alexandra, "Some People Want to Cancel Skai Jackson after She 'Doxed' a 13-Year-Old," *Daily Dot,* June 2020. Accessed December 23, 2021. https://www.dailydot.com/irl/skai-jackson-dox/.

16. Witt, Lara, "I Was Doxxed By White Supremacists for Stepping Out of Line," *I Was Doxxed By White Supremacists for Stepping Out of Line,* May 2021. Accessed June 17, 2021. https://www.wearyourvoicemag.com/i-was-doxxed-by-white-supremacists-for-stepping-out-of-line/.

17. Blanch and Hsu, "An Introduction to Violent Crime on the Internet."

18. Blanch and Hsu, "An Introduction to Violent Crime on the Internet," 6.

19. boyd, danah, "Truth, Lies, and 'Doxxing': The Real Moral of the Gawker/Reddit Story," *Wired,* 2012. Accessed August 31, 2021. https://www.wired.com/2012/10/truth-lies-doxxing-internet-vigilanteism/.

20. Williams, "Ostracism: The Kiss of Social Death."

21. Williams, Apryl, "Black Memes Matter: #LivingWhileBlack with Becky and Karen," *Social Media + Society* 6 (2020): 2056305120981047. doi: 10.1177/2056305120981047

22. Williams, "Black Memes Matter: #LivingWhileBlack with Becky and Karen," 1.

23. Brown, Dalvin, "Twitter's Cancel Culture: A Force for Good or a Digital Witchhunt? The Answer Is Complicated," *USA Today,* July 2020. Accessed April 14, 2021. https://www.usatoday.com/story/tech/2020/07/17/has-twitters-cancel-culture-gone-too-far/5445804002/.

24. Staff writers, Knowyourmeme.com, "Dog Poo Girl," *Know Your Meme,* 2005. Accessed December 23, 2021. https://knowyourmeme.com/memes/dog-poo-girl.

25. Wulfson, Joseph A., "College Professor Fired For Posting Online That Otto Warmbier 'Got What He Deserved,'" *Mediaite,* 2017. Accessed December 23, 2021. https://www.mediaite.com/online/college-professor-fired-for-posting-online-that-otto-warmbier-got-what-he-deserved/.

26. Králová, Jana, "What Is Social Death?" *Contemporary Social Science* 10 (2015): 235–248.

27. Patterson, Orlando, *Slavery and Social Death: A Comparative Study* (Harvard University Press, 1982).

28. Williams, "Ostracism: The Kiss of Social Death."

29. Foucault, Michel, *Discipline and Punish: The Birth of the Prison* (New York: Vintage Books, a division of Random House, 1979), 17.

30. Patterson, *Slavery and Social Death.*

31. Defender Staff, "South Korea Draws up Cyberbulling Laws after Second K-Pop Suicide," *DMCA Defender,* December 2019. Accessed January 15, 2020. http://dmcadefender.com/south-korea-draws-up-cyberbulling-laws-after-second-k-pop-suicide/.

32. Durkheim, Emil, *The Division of Labor in Society* (New York: Free Press, 1964).

33. Durkheim, *The Division of Labor in Society.*

34. Dugas, Michelle, and Arie W. Kruglanski, "The Quest for Significance Model of Radicalization: Implications for the Management of Terrorist Detainees," *Behavioral Sciences & the Law* 32 (2014): 423–439. doi: 10.1002/bsl.2122.

35. Kruglanski, Arie W., Jocelyn J. Bélanger, and Rohan Gunaratna, *The Three Pillars of Radicalization: Needs, Narratives, and Networks* (Oxford University Press, 2019).

36. Kruglanski, Arie W., Jocelyn J. Bélanger, Michele Gelfand, Rohan Gunaratna, Malkanthi Hettiarachchi, Fernando Reinares, Edward Orehek, Jo Sasota, and Keren Sharvit, "Terrorism—A (Self) Love Story: Redirecting the Significance Quest Can End Violence," *American Psychologist* 68 (2013): 559–575. doi: 10.1037/a0032615.

37. Rogan, Randall G., "Acknowledgment as a Primary Motive for Violent Extremism," unpublished manuscript, Wake Forest, NC, 2018.

38. Rogan, Randall G., "Quest for Immortality: An Analysis of ISIS's Dabiq," *International Journal of Communication* 13 (2019): 20.

39. Becker, Ernest, *The Birth and Death of Meaning: A Perspective in Psychiatry and Anthropology* (New York: Free Press of Glencoe, 1962).

40. Kruglanski, Bélanger, and Gunaratna, *The Three Pillars of Radicalization.*

41. Rogan, "Acknowledgment as a Primary Motive for Violent Extremism."

42. Rogan, "Acknowledgment as a Primary Motive for Violent Extremism."

43. Becker, *The Birth and Death of Meaning.*

44. Becker, *The Birth and Death of Meaning.*

45. Becker, *The Birth and Death of Meaning.*

46. Kruglanski, Bélanger et al., "Terrorism—A (Self) Love Story."

47. Rogan, "Acknowledgment as a Primary Motive for Violent Extremism."

48. Rogan, "Acknowledgment as a Primary Motive for Violent Extremism."

49. Becker, *The Birth and Death of Meaning.*

50. Dugas, Michelle, and Arie W. Kruglanski, "The Quest for Significance Model of Radicalization: Implications for the Management of Terrorist Detainees," *Behavioral Sciences & the Law* 32 (2014): 423–439.

51. Kruglanski, Bélanger et al., "Terrorism—A (Self) Love Story."

52. Rogan, "Acknowledgment as a Primary Motive for Violent Extremism."

53. Becker, *The Birth and Death of Meaning.*

54. Becker, *The Birth and Death of Meaning*, 77.

55. Becker, *The Birth and Death of Meaning.*

56. Becker, *The Birth and Death of Meaning*, 124.

57. Becker, *The Birth and Death of Meaning*, 124.

58. Castillo, Bernal Diaz Del, *The Conquest of New Spain,* translated by John M. Cohen (London: Penguin Books, 1521/1963).

59. Osborn, Alex, *Your Creative Power: How to Use Imagination* (New York: Scribner, 1949).

60. McLuhan, M., Fiore, Q., and Agel, J., *The Medium Is the Massage: An Inventory of Effects* (San Francisco: HardWired, 1966).

61. McLuhan et al., *The Medium Is the Massage*, 7.

62. Becker, *The Birth and Death of Meaning.*

63. Rogan, "Acknowledgment as a Primary Motive for Violent Extremism."

64. Vaidhyanathan, Sica, *Antisocial Media: How Facebook Disconnects Us and Undermines Democracy* (Oxford: Oxford University Press, 2018).

65. Rheingold, Howard, *Smart Mobs: The Next Social Revolution* (Cambridge, MA: Perseus Publications, 2002).
66. Rheingold, *Smart Mobs*, 170.
67. Rheingold, *Smart Mobs*, xii.
68. Rheingold, *Smart Mobs*, xvii.
69. Rheingold, *Smart Mobs*, xvii.
70. Rheingold, *Smart Mobs*, 185.
71. Rheingold, *Smart Mobs*, 185.
72. Vaidhyanathan, *Antisocial Media.*
73. Brown, Dalvin, "Twitter's Cancel Culture: A Force for Good or a Digital Witchhunt? The Answer Is Complicated," *USA Today*, 17 July 2020. https://www.usatoday.com/story/tech/2020/07/17/has-twitters-cancel-culture-gone-too-far/5445804002/.
74. Flood, Allison, "Young Adult Author Cancels Own Novel after Race Controversy," *The Guardian*, February 1, 2019. Accessed April 14, 2021. http://www.theguardian.com/books/2019/feb/01/young-adult-author-cancels-own-novel-after-race-controversy.
75. Wulfson, "College Professor Fired for Posting Online that Otto Warmbier 'Got What He Deserved.'"
76. Lijphart, Arend, *Democracy in Plural Societies: A Comparative Exploration* (New Haven: Yale University Press, 1977).
77. Andeweg, Rudy B., "Consociationalism." In *International Encyclopedia of the Social & Behavioral Sciences* (2nd edition), edited by James D. Wright, 692–694 (Oxford: Elsevier, 2015).
78. Solove, Daniel, "Balkinization: Of Privacy and Poop: Norm Enforcement Via the Blogosphere," *Balkin Blog,* 2005. Accessed December 22, 2021. https://balkin.blogspot.com/2005/06/of-privacy-and-poop-norm-enforcement.html.
79. Staff writers, *Know Your Meme*, "Dog Poo Girl."
80. Bentham, Jeremy, *Panopticon, or the Inspection House* (London: T. Payne, 1791).
81. Foucault, *Discipline and Punish,* 201.
82. Foucault, *Discipline and Punish,* 206.
83. Ronson, Jon, *So You've Been Publicly Shamed* (New York: Penguin Publishing Group, 2015).
84. Foucault, *Discipline and Punish,* 201.
85. "Black Teen Speaks Out after Woman Is Charged with Attacking Him at Pool," *CBS News,* 2018. Accessed July 22, 2022. https://www.cbsnews.com/news/pool-patrol-paula-story-black-teen-dj-simmons-speaks-out-assault-stephanie-sebby-strempel/.
86. "'BBQ Becky,' White Woman Who Called Cops on Black BBQ, 911 Tapes Released: 'I'm Really Scared! Come Quick!'" *Newsweek*, September 4, 2018.
87. Solove, Daniel J., "Shaming and the Digital Scarlet Letter." In *The Future of Reputation*, 76–102 (New Haven: Yale University Press, 2007).

88. Writers, and Free Expression Team, "PEN Case Study: Salman Rushdie," *Writers and Free Expression Blog,* 2018. Accessed December 25, 2021. https://writersandfreeexpression.com/2018/04/23/pen-case-study-salman-rushdie/.

89. Writers, and Free Expression Team, "PEN Case Study: Salman Rushdie."

90. Hafezi, Parisa, "Iranian Media Outlets Add to Bounty for Killing Britain's Rushdie," *Reuters,* 2016. Accessed December 25, 2021. https://www.reuters.com/article/us-iran-rushdie/iranian-media-outlets-add-to-bounty-for-killing-britains-rushdie-idUSKCN0VV1TI.

91. Tharoor, Ishaan, "Nobel Organization Decides to Condemn the Fatwa Against Salman Rushdie, 27 Years Later," *The Washington Post,* March 4, 2016.

Chapter 2

Instilling Terror On- and Offline

HOW THE ONLINE AND OFFLINE ENVIRONMENTS INFLUENCE ONE ANOTHER

In chapter 1, I explored how the quest for acknowledgment can motivate online conflicts. Fame seeking has its root in the quest for acknowledgment and escalating conflicts online emerge as a defense against perceived existential threats to the participants' world views. This chapter focuses on whether and how the offline *real* physical world and the online *virtual* world interact and affect one another, often in ways we cannot control that lead to devastating consequences.

All too often, people who engage online are lulled into believing the internet and social media provide anonymity, or that the virtual and physical worlds are somehow separated, insulated from each other, providing a free space for engaging with impunity. But these parallel worlds always have a reciprocal relationship, and what occurs online has direct impact on the quality of our physical lives.

VARIETIES OF ON- AND OFFLINE RELATIONSHIPS

The sequence of events taking place alternately on- and offline varies. One of the most common types of social media conflict scenarios occurs when onlookers encounter an event in the physical world—one they are not necessarily involved in—and they record it with the specific intent of posting it on social media, usually to shame someone involved in the conflict they believe is at fault. Others who view the posting then escalate the shaming by reposting the recording. I call this shaming activity "the digital pillory," a phrase borrowed from Hess and Waller[1] reminiscent of the public punishments of medieval England. In so doing, sometimes third parties who view the shaming posts continue to shame and target long after the initial uploader and target have forgotten the conflict. Scandals that go up on the internet and social media are permanent. In some cases, hate groups take over the narrative and use it to their own ends, to spread hate online and recruit members.

Another social media conflict scenario starts online and people who identify the actors take the conflict offline, sometimes with dire physical consequences. This is the case of neighborhood gang rivalries detailed in Geoffrey Lane's ethnography *The Digital Street*.[2] In this interesting ethnography, there is a reciprocal relationship between events on social media and on the street. A third scenario occurs when violent groups carefully plan and produce videos of their cruelty and post the videos online to create psychological terror, knowing that the videos will go viral. Some use the posts or videos to recruit members, as I detail in the events about ISIS terrorists. The fourth scenario for social media conflict occurs when individuals or groups use real-time streaming to livestream heinous acts. In this case, online and offline are blended in time, and the world watches helplessly as the violent acts unfold. The events in Christchurch, New Zealand, of the tragic killing at two separate mosques by the same killer describe this phenomenon.

THE DIGITAL PILLORY

Although many online conflicts begin and stay online, one of the most common digital conflict scenarios is the result of pictures and videos taken by observers to record events taking place offline and posting the images to social media to shame the protagonist. The uploading onto social media of offline offenses is the modern equivalent of real-world public punishments that have occurred over the course of human history. In medieval England, for example, public punishments were a part of the legal process, serving as a deterrent to others in the community.[3] Similarly in Puritan New England, close-knit communities would shame the accused by placing them in a position of humiliation using tools such as the pillory, stocks, or barrel.[4]

The public pillory was abolished throughout most of Great Britain, for example, by the late 1830s "not because they were ineffective, but because they were far too brutal."[5] Today, however, the public pillory has returned digitally because people, no matter where they flee to, can be singled out, identified through internet searches and social media with pictures and videos, and punished in perpetuity. Moving to a new, crowded city to "blend into the woodwork" is no longer possible.

THE CASE OF THE "STOLEN" CELLPHONE AND THE SHAMING THAT FOLLOWED

One example of the digital pillory, told by Daniel Solove in his book *The Future of Reputation*,[6] took place in 2005, during the early days of social media when a man's cellphone was stolen. The cellphone company had provided a specific website to each cellphone owner on which to upload photos and videos. When the man looked up the website a few days after his phone was stolen, he saw about 40 new photos taken by a young man driving a car. Believing this was the person who stole his cellphone, he wrote the young man, threatening to plaster the pictures around the town, and he then carried out his threat.[7]

The photos went viral and link to the photos, with the young man labeled as a thief, circulated throughout the world. People responded with comments urging maximum punishment and further circulating the young man's picture because they believed he needed to be taught a lesson. The comments beneath the pictures became outrageously cruel, and one person produced a meme, a wanted poster with the alleged thief's face on it.[8]

After posting the man's photos, the theft victim decided to report the theft to law enforcement. Upon investigation, the police determined that the young man was still a minor and urged the theft victim to remove the minor's name from his website. But, when he did as the police asked, the other website users who had been urging for the thief to be punished turned on the theft victim. They stated that they would go on posting the boy's name and face and calling him a thief to punish him. Additional personal information about the young man was subsequently posted on the website.[9] To make matters worse, the personal information of several people with the same name as the young man were posted publicly.[10]

The persistent attacks against the young man surprised the theft victim and made him feel remorseful, but it was too late. The digital pillory had already taken off and, once the information had been released, it was impossible to control. The young man became a viral scapegoat for theft even though doing so was against the law.

THIRD-PARTY ONLINE HATEMONGERS: NEO-NAZIS USING THE INTERNET TO TERRORIZE AND RECRUIT

The punishments in the "phone theft" case were harsh, and both the theft and the online punishing behaviors were illegal. But those cases arose from a moral conviction that the culprit had stolen, and therefore morally transgressed against the cellphone owner. Internet users who continued with cyber harassment did so from a place of moral conviction against theft. The cell-phone case, too, thankfully did not result in serious physical harm, though it could have. There are, however, instances where third-party hate groups not only engage in digital hatemongering passed off as a moral worldview, but, like some terrorist groups such as ISIS, they weaponize the internet to foment what could be construed as an act of cyberterrorism against their victims. As Rogan[11] and Kruglanski et al.[12] have explained for terrorist groups, these online hate groups too act out of a desire for acknowledgment of a moral worldview that, although hateful, abhorrent, and untenable, are adhered to by their members fervently enough to wage domestic warfare against their perceived enemies.

One of the most notorious cases of using social media to punish people is Andrew Anglin who in 2016 used his neo-Nazi website, the *Daily Die Sturmer*, and is considered the leading extremist website in the country.[13]

A realtor targeted by Anglin became involved when residents of the town organized to oppose the planned use of Whitefish for a conference of white supremacists being organized by the notorious Richard Spencer. The venue selected for the conference was a commercial building owned by Spencer's mother, Sherry Spencer.

Fearing the town's good name would become associated with white nationalism, the community petitioned the Whitefish City Hall for an anti-hate ordinance. In addition, Mrs. Spencer's tenants urged her to sell the building. After that Mrs. Spencer contacted the realtor and, after discussing whether to sell, the realtor agreed to help Mrs. Spencer do so.[14]

Days later, after the owner told her son about the sale, Mrs. Spencer informed the realtor she had decided to go with a different agent. Some days later Mrs. Spencer wrote a scathing blog article about the realtor, alleging that members of a local anti-hate group *Love Lives Here* had told her that if she did not sell the building, about 200 protesters would descend on Whitefish and that would drive down property values.[15,16,17]

Anglin seized upon the blog post to encourage his neo-Nazi supporters to teach the Jewish realtor a lesson. Using ugly antisemitic tropes and holocaust references, he wrote nearly 30 articles defaming the realtor. He also issued a "call to arms" to his followers to unleash a "troll storm" against the realtor, her husband, and their 12-year-old son.[18,19,20]

In an illegal act of doxing, Anglin published the realtor's email addresses and social media profiles, as well as her and her family's telephone numbers. The family's presence on social media for business and pleasure facilitated the neo-Nazis' ability to target them by leaving violent comments on their account and feeds. Using Nazi propaganda and imagery, Anglin demanded that his followers confront the realtor and ". . . take action against her Jewish agenda."[21,22,23,24]

Over a matter of weeks, the realtor, her husband, and her son received well over 700 threats, via texts, snail mail, email, and voicemail.[25,26] The communications included death threats, holocaust references, misogynist rants, menacing Christmas cards, and ethnic slurs.[27]

Anglin's followers contacted the realtor's office, her husband's office, and her son's cellphone and targeted Jewish and Jewish-sounding brick-and-mortar businesses in Whitefish. Anglin threatened to descend on Whitefish with his hordes in busloads, armed and ready to march against the Jews.[28,29] Although Anglin later canceled the march, he had opened the door to the prospect of violence in the real world, including in person against the realtor. He used his digital platform and his access to social media to transition this concerted action from the virtual to the physical world.

Anglin exploited the *Love Lives Here* campaign to scapegoat the Jewish realtor, create publicity, and recruit followers. In the Whitefish case and others since he has encouraged fellow neo-Nazis to be at the ready to launch attacks on people he has determined deserve punishment.

The realtor incident was an astonishing cascade of on- and offline events that involved a national hate group coopting a local conflict—albeit with national implications—to arbitrarily inflict pain, social and physical death on one family using online platforms.

When the threats had besieged the realtor's family, the realtor and her family turned to the Southern Poverty Law Center (SPLC) in what became the SPLC's first digital hate case. Their lawsuit against Anglin won a $14 million judgment in favor of the realtor for intimidation, defamation, and invasion of privacy.[30] Anglin fled the country to avoid payment.[31]

The Whitefish case illustrates that digital punishment, whether intended to impose a tyrannical worldview or to terrorize and recruit, is exceedingly dangerous. The punishments, therefore, go forward in an environment that lacks deliberative factfinding and investigation. The impacts are real world and the errors in many, if not most, cases cannot be corrected.

Another case occurred in the aftermath of the 2016 "Unite the Right" rally in Charlottesville, Virginia, an event organized by a mix of white supremacists, neo-Nazis, and Confederacy sympathizers.[32] The marchers, intent on terrorizing and recruiting, came prepared for violence and that's what happened. One woman was killed by a car driven into a crowd of counter-protesters, and scores of others were severely injured.

In the outrage that followed the rally, many began reviewing the pictures and videos taken during the march to identify and shame the culprits. One of the marchers who had been recorded shouting slogans like "Jews will not replace us!" was wearing a T-shirt from the Engineering School at the University of Arkansas. The online "sleuths" misidentified an assistant professor of engineering at that university who coincidentally resembled the man in the Charlottesville march photos. The professor was attacked online and received death threats. He had to stay with a friend for several weeks until the public was convinced that he was not, in fact, at the march and that the person in the photo was not he (Victor 2017, Sydell 2017).[33,34]

In Another online-offline interaction, conflict begins online but migrates offline because the people involved can identify one another and live close enough to approach each other in the physical world. Jeffrey Lane's ethnography *The Digital Street*[35] analyzed the interaction between the physical and virtual worlds of at-risk youth at a Harlem ministry, the Peace Ministry of Pastor Jeffrey Canada. Lane found that the proliferation of digital technologies among the youth, especially smartphones, resulted in an online world that paralleled the physical world the youth inhabited, including its actors, cultural references, and the issues they grappled with. These two milieus shaped one another and were shaped by one another.

Pastor Canada realized the connectedness of these two worlds when a sudden, seemingly unexplained shooting between two rival groups occurred in his neighborhood. Upon investigation, he found that boys from different physical neighborhoods and gangs were linked together on social media by the same girls. The boys had an argument about the girls who came to blows on the physical street. With this incident, Pastor Canada realized that mentoring and adult supervision online were just as crucial as physical disciplinary and character-building measures.

Lane's study concluded that the technology both empowered and constrained the youth. He found that the perceived anonymity of social media by the youth induced them to "try on" different virtual identities, and he found that the youth got into unexpected conflicts that grew antagonistic and led to street violence. Lastly, the digital breadcrumbs the youth left behind eased tracking by law enforcement, arrest, and incarceration. These factors made the virtual world precarious for the youth.

The youth at the Harlem Youth Ministry were easily identified by law enforcement, an indication that the internet is not an anonymous platform. Social media technologies provide multiple, overlapping methods of identifying users, from their IP address to their device IMEI numbers, to the Wi-Fi networks they are standing near to. It is, therefore, extremely difficult to remain anonymous online even for the most sophisticated user of social media.

The quest for acknowledgment by inner-city youth, and the uncensored postings that the quest inspired, inevitably escalated into online conflicts that were finished off in the street, ending in death. Most importantly, had the youth not been online, the conflicts might not have surfaced in the first place, or at least not surfaced as quickly as face-to-face conflict. There would also be far fewer breadcrumbs for law enforcement to follow. So, contrary to Lane's conclusion, the "empowerment?" the youths believed they had attained through social media use was illusory.

PLANNING OF CRUEL ACTS ESPECIALLY FOR THE INTERNET

In addition to online groups jumping offline to punish others, as in the Lane ethnography, sometimes online actors jump on- and offline to terrorize and recruit. The Whitefish incident and "Unite the Right" rally both had these elements. Sometimes, malicious lone wolfs commit heinous acts knowing full well they may end up in a video on the internet as the objects of abhorrence.

On Sunday, March 10, 2019, at 3:10 am, for example, on a subway near Harlem, a heinous act was video recorded and uploaded by bystanders at the request of the criminal. The video showed a middle-aged man standing in the subway car striking repeated roundhouse kicks to the head and upper body of a 78-year-old woman. None of the onlookers intervened.

Before leaving the subway car, the assailant shouted "Worldstar that!"[36] He was referring to the Worldstarhiphop.com website where violent videos are sometimes posted. This was an abhorrent act that the perpetrator fully expected would be uploaded somewhere, somehow, because his crime was so cruel and heinous that he caused multiple people to record the incident on their smartphones for reporting to law enforcement and, yes, posting on social media.

Some reports indicated that the woman had said something to incite the assailant's anger. But did he carry out the attack to end up on the internet? The video clearly showed his depravity, but did he have such deep-seated cruelty because of a need for acknowledgment? As expected, NYPD identified and located the attacker, and he was placed under arrest shortly afterward (McNamara 2019).[37] This man on the subway was a disturbed person acting alone, and it is not clear if he had planned the action several minutes before, or if something suddenly precipitated his cruel assault on the elderly woman. Nevertheless, his statement makes clear that he intended take an offline action online in order to be the center of attention.

CURATED TERRORISM: ISIS' HEINOUS "MOVIES"

The phenomenon of posting violence also happened with Middle Eastern terrorist groups whose planning of bizarre, stylized heinousness is unsurpassed. ISIS, for example, committed inhumane acts on the ground, videotaped them, and edited them into full-blown productions with credits and soundtracks before releasing them online, assuming correctly that they would go viral. These surreal, grotesque videos were planned for the purpose of terrorizing the public, attracting violent recruits, and gaining acknowledgment and followers.

On February 3, 2015, for example, ISIS released a 22-minute video on social media depicting the forced confession, "trial," and live-burning—in a cage—of a captured Jordanian fighter pilot.[38] The gruesome propaganda video featured narration, sound effects, and logo art. The video was subsequently released to ISIS' social media accounts—yes, they had them—and went viral. ISIS demanded that viewers conform to their unfathomable fundamentalist worldview or be punished in the same manner as the live-burned officer.

With this act, ISIS, a genocidal group, had turned morality and human rights norms on their heads.[39] The actions of ISIS harken back to the era of medieval torture, but its leaders understood that digital technology and social media were completely consonant with advancing their medieval worldview. They saw absolutely no conflict with using ultramodern technology to advance ancient battles because it is so conducive to enabling their barbaric brand to go viral, and so fulfilling of their need and desire to be acknowledged as a significant player on the world stage.

LIVESTREAMING TERRORISM AND SLAUGHTER: ONLINE AND OFFLINE MEET

The ISIS video was prerecorded and uploaded. But recent technology has allowed others to get even more acknowledgment and shock value with audiences who know terror is about to happen but are unable to stop it. In these cases, the interaction between online and offline events is in real time.

One example of this was a tragic mass shooting in New Zealand. The incident took place in 2018, just two years after Facebook CEO Mark Zuckerberg—realizing that he was losing the younger demographic to Snapchat—decided to incorporate live video on his platform, calling the service Facebook Live. Facebook deployed the technology within two months of Snapchat's launch, paying scant attention to its social ramifications.[40]

In the New Zealand mass shooting case, a vicious lone gunman, 29-year-old Australian terrorist Brenton Tarrant, livestreamed himself on Facebook murdering 51 people at 2 separate mosques in Christchurch, New Zealand.[41] For some time before the attack, Tarrant had been active on the unmonitored chat platform 8chan. During the incident, Tarrant was in his car with a cache of weapons and racist music blaring. He depicted in detail, from a first-person perspective, the mass killing of men, women, and children, even going back and forth to his vehicle to reload weapons and show his meticulous planning and execution.

Tarrant appeared to share these horrific acts of extreme violence to glorify himself. He even provided verbal "how to" instructions to viewers in a cool, neutral manner.[42] And he included white supremacist symbolism in his video. For example, the song he played is called "Kabab Remover," a racist song created by Serbian soldiers during the Serbian massacres of 1992–1996.[43,44] His firearm sported the number 14, likely standing for a 14-word mantra used by some white supremacists groups "We must secure the existence of our people and a future for white children."[45] Having rolled out Facebook Live relatively quickly, the company did not have sufficient artificial intelligence to flag live mass shootings. The footage was too complex. It also too closely resembled video games (Kan 2019, Hoyle and Rhiannon 2019, 2017).[46,47] Consequently, as casualties amassed that day, nearly 4,000 people watched the killing of scores of people live on Facebook before it was taken down.[48]

SOCIAL MEDIA BUSINESS MODEL AND ALGORITHMS ENCOURAGE ABUSE

Facebook's premature release of Facebook Live cost the New Zealand shooting victims many lives. But technology is often rolled out too quickly. Eric Klinenberg has written in *The Nation* that the real reason for making so many half-baked tools available to the public is that social media's true intention is to maintain consumers on their platform at any cost, rather than encouraging face-to-face interaction.[49,50] The human connections needed to escape danger, establish trust and safety, and rebuild society require recurrent social interaction in physical places, not pokes and likes with online "friends." So, it is inevitable, given the potential to brew so much more conflict than the prospect of promoting new, deeper relationships, that live video platforms will be abused for grandstanding and worse, human atrocity.

As early as 2017, for example, activists against digital crime cautioned that Facebook Live would have the potential to be abused by criminal gangs and others seeking to get attention. Jane Hitchcock, an activist for the Working Group to Halt Online Abuse, stated that many criminals would turn to Facebook Live to publicize their acts. She noted that in 2017, a mother in Ohio taped her toddler to the wall while she did housework and live streamed the act. In addition, a mother in Georgia beat her daughter live on Facebook Live.[51]

Livestreaming is the ultimate near instant interaction between on- and offline milieus. As more real-time streaming platforms are rolled out, the online social media panopticon, and opportunities for digital pillory, will become ever more present. At the heart of these cases of online cruelty is technology that enables the actors to obtain near instantaneous fame and the acknowledgment they crave—and if we do not establish effective guardrails, we can expect to see more.

WHY DID I POST THAT?

Last, there is the issue of posts that users make on their own volition, not knowing the immediate or future repercussions. As I mentioned in chapter 1, a significant problem that stops us from subduing the digital pillory is the permanence of posts on the internet.[52] This is especially notable when posts that have remained online for years return to haunt people. In these cases, the people have changed, but the information they have posted has not.

One of the more common ways that permanence ruins lives is people who lose jobs and job offers because of offensive postings that are years or even decades old. This occurred to two notable African Americans fired from newly earned positions in Hollywood and the media.

In 2018, comedian Kevin Hart was given the job of hosting the Oscars. But homophobic tweets emerged from 2009 when one of his comedy skits focused on how he would try to stop his son from "being gay."[53]

In the years that followed, Hart apologized for his homophobia and changed his comedy routines considerably. But when the story resurfaced in 2018, Hart was asked by the Oscars to publicly apologize, which he did, and he withdrew from hosting the Oscars. After that, Brian Raftery of *Wired* magazine quipped that Hart had not lost the job because of the tweets, but rather because of the obtuse way he apologized.[54]

But other cases involving the unforgiving nature of the internet have demonstrated that the main problem is precisely the remnants of old postings. African American political commentator and reporter Alexi McCammond of Axios News found that the problem is the technology, not the apology. McCammond, aged 27, had been offered the position of editor-in-chief for *Teen Vogue*. Sometime earlier, internet norm enforcers had found anti-Asian and homophobic tweets she had posted when she was 17. Her new employer was aware of these tweets and believed that the public would be satisfied with Alexi's multiple prior and present apologies about the tweets. But the digital pillory was relentless, and the job offer was rescinded shortly after it was offered.[55,56,57]

As we come to reconsider the repercussions of posting controversial material to the internet to receive acknowledgment, it is helpful to consider whether we are setting ourselves up for future offline punishment for something we posted online many years prior.

NOTES

1. Hess, Kristy, and Lisa Waller, "The Digital Pillory: Media Shaming of 'Ordinary' People for Minor Crimes," *Continuum* 28, no. 1 (2014): 101–111.
2. Lane, Jeffery, *The Digital Street* (New York: Oxford University Press, 2008).
3. Solove, Daniel, *The Future of Reputation: Gossip, Rumor, and Privacy on the Internet* (New Haven: Yale University Press 2007).
4. New England Historical Society, "Way More Than the Scarlet Letter: Puritan Punishments," *New England Historical Society,* 2015. Accessed March 13, 2019. http://www.newenglandhistoricalsociety.com/way-more-than-the-scarlet-letter-puritan-punishments/.
5. Lewis, Helen, "Against the Rage Machine," *New Statesman* 144 (2017): 43.
6. Solove, *The Future of Reputation.*
7. Solove, *The Future of Reputation.*
8. Solove, *The Future of Reputation.*
9. Solove, *The Future of Reputation.*
10. Solove, *The Future of Reputation.*
11. Rogan, Randall, "Acknowledgment as a Primary Motive for Violent Extremism," unpublished manuscript, Wake Forest, NC, 2018.
12. Kruglanski, Arie W., Jocelyn J. Bélanger, and Rohan Gunaratna, "Significance Quest Theory of Radicalization." In *The Three Pillars of Radicalization* (New York: Oxford University Press, 2019).
13. Hankes, Keegan, "Eye of the Stormer," *Southern Poverty Law Center Intelligence Report,* 2017. Accessed December 21, 2021. https://www.splcenter.org/fighting-hate/intelligence-report/2017/eye-stormer.
14. Beckett, Lois, "How Richard Spencer's Home Town Weathered a Neo-Nazi 'Troll Storm,'" *The Guardian,* 2017. Accessed December 26, 2021. https://www.theguardian.com/us-news/2017/feb/05/richard-spencer-whitefish-neo-nazi-march.
15. Nashrullah, Tasneem, "Neo-Nazis Target Jewish Families in White Nationalist Leader's Hometown," *Buzzfeednews.com,* December 2016. Accessed June 1, 2021. https://www.buzzfeednews.com/article/tasneemnashrulla/neo-nazis-target-jewish-families-and-establishments-in-monta.
16. Weisman, Jonathan, *(Semitism): Being Jewish in America in the Age of Trump* (New York: St. Martin's Press, 2018).
17. Hankes, "Eye of the Stormer."
18. Lenz, Ryan, "A Gathering of Eagles: Extremists Look to Montana," *Southern Poverty Law Center Intelligence Report,* 2011. Accessed August 7, 2021. https://www.splcenter.org/fighting-hate/intelligence-report/2011/gathering-eagles-extremists-look-montana.
19. Mullin, Joe, "Lawsuit: Neo-Nazi Website Owner Is Liable for Harassing Montana Real Estate Agent," *Arstechnica.com,* 2017. Accessed August 2, 2021. https://arstechnica.com/tech-policy/2017/04/neo-nazi-website-that-launched-a-troll-storm-is-sued-for-harassment/.
20. Hankes, "Eye of the Stormer."

21. Sankin, Aaron. "Where in the World Is America's Leading Neo-Nazi Troll?" *Revealnews.org*, July 2017. Accessed December 21, 2021. http://revealnews.org/blog/where-in-the-world-is-americas-leading-neo-nazi-troll/.

22. Lenz, "A Gathering of Eagles: Extremists Look to Montana."

23. Mullin, "Lawsuit: Neo-Nazi Website Owner Is Liable for Harassing Montana Real Estate Agent."

24. Hankes, "Eye of the Stormer."

25. Lenz, "A Gathering of Eagles: Extremists Look to Montana."

26. Hankes, "Eye of the Stormer."

27. Mullin, "Lawsuit: Neo-Nazi Website Owner Is Liable for Harassing Montana Real Estate Agent."

28. Mullin, "Lawsuit: Neo-Nazi Website Owner Is Liable for Harassing Montana Real Estate Agent."

29. SPLC, "Eye of the Stormer," *Eye of the Stormer.*

30. Hankes, "Eye of the Stormer."

31. Padilla, Mariel, "Daily Stormer Founder Should Pay 'Troll Storm' Victim $14 Million, Judge Says," *New York Times.* July 16, 2019.

32. MacFarquhar, Neil, "Jury Finds Rally Organizers Responsible for Charlottesville Violence," *The New York Times,* 2021.

33. Victor, Daniel, "Amateur Sleuths Aim to Identify Charlottesville Marchers, but Sometimes Misfire," *The New York Times,* August 15, 2017.

34. Sydell, Laura, "Kyle Quinn Hid at a Friend's House After Being Misidentified on Twitter as a Racist," *NPR News,* August 15, 2017.

35. Lane, *The Digital Street.*

36. Howard, Brooke L. "NYPD Seeks Tips After Vicious Subway Attack Caught on Video," *The Daily Beast,* March 22, 2019.

37. McNamara, Audrey, "NYPD Catches Suspect in Brutal Subway Attack of Elderly Woman," *Thedailybeast.com,* April 30, 2019.

38. ISIS, "Warning, Extremely Graphic Video: ISIS Burns Hostage Alive," *Foxnews.com,* 2015. Accessed June 24, 2019. http://video.foxnews.com/v/4030583977001/.

39. ISIS, "Isis Burns Hostage Alive."

40. Hern, Alex, "Facebook Live Is Changing the World - But Not in the Way It Hoped," *The Guardian,* January 5, 2017.

41. Macklin, Graham, "The Christchurch Attacks: Livestream Terror in the Viral Video Age," *Combatting Terrorism Center at West Point,* July 2019. Accessed August 7, 2021. https://ctc.usma.edu/christchurch-attacks-livestream-terror-viral-video-age/.

42. Macklin, "The Christchurch Attacks: Livestream Terror in the Viral Video Age."

43. Unknown author, "Serbia Strong / Remove Kebab," *Know Your Meme,* 2010. Accessed August 9, 2021. https://knowyourmeme.com/memes/serbia-strong-remove-kebab.

44. Macklin, "The Christchurch Attacks: Livestream Terror in the Viral Video Age."

45. Anti-Defamation League Staff. "14 Words." ADL.ORG, 3 May 2022. https://www.adl.org/resources/hate-symbol/14-words.

46. Kan, Michael, "Why Facebook's AI Failed to Detect Video of New Zealand Shooting," *PC Magazine,* 2019. Accessed June 25, 2019. https://www.pcmag.com/news/367318/why-facebooks-ai-failed-to-detect-video-of-new-zealand-shoo.

47. Hoyle, Rhiannon, and Niharika Mandhana, "Facebook Left Up Video of New Zealand Shootings for an Hour," *Wall Street Journal,* March 21, 2019.

48. Feiner, Lauren, "Facebook Explains Why Its A.I. Didn't Detect the New Zealand Mosque Shooting Video Before It Was Viewed 4,000 Times," *CNBC.com,* March 21, 2019.

49. Klinenberg, Eric, "Social Media Can't Replace Social Infrastructure," *The Nation,* May 2, 2019.

50. Phillips, Whitney, "The Oxygen of Amplification," *Data and Society,* May 2018. Accessed December 27, 2021. https://datasociety.net/library/oxygen-of-amplification/.

51. French, Laura. "The Social Media Age: More Suicides, Violent Acts Streamed Live," *Forensic Magazine,* February 2, 2017.

52. Solove, *The Future of Reputation.*

53. Daw, Stephen, "A Complete Timeline of Kevin Hart's Oscar-Hosting Controversy, From Tweets to Apologies," *Billboard.com,* January 13, 2020.

54. Raftery, Brian, "Kevin Hart's Tweets Didn't Doom Him—His Messy Apology Did," *Wired,* December 7, 2018.

55. Ellefson, Lindsey, "Alexi McCammond Returns to MSNBC After Teen Vogue Exit (Video)," *The Wrap,* May 13, 2021.

56. Haring, Bruce, "Alexi McCammond Returns To Axios As Political Reporter," *Deadline,* July 3, 2021.

57. Robertson, Katie, "Teen Vogue Staff Members Condemn Editor's Decade-Old, Racist Tweets," *The New York Times,* May 9, 2021.

Chapter 3

When Images Lie

On the early evening of January 18, 2019, a 24-second video was shot that emerged on Twitter the following day showing a Native American man named Nathan Phillips chanting and drumming close to the face of an American white teenager wearing a red, Trump Campaign "Make America Great Again" (MAGA) cap.[1] The boy's name, it was found, was Nick Sandmann. But for the occasional smile on his face, Nick was very still. He was also surrounded by a throng of other students, all male, hollering and enervated, and doing "tomahawk chops." But they did not approach Phillips. Some of the other students were wearing "MAGA" caps. Before long, most mainstream media interpreted the video as that of racist White young men mocking, disrespecting, and attacking the Native American man.[2,3,4,5,6]

The only known facts about the video at the time of its release were that the March for Life, an anti-abortion march, coincided with the Indigenous Peoples' March, and toward the end of the day, tired people—from both politically and highly dissimilar groups—awaited their buses and other means to go home in a common area near the steps of the Lincoln Memorial. Although the "March for Life" ended 3–4 hours earlier than when the video was taken and was near the opposite end of the Mall, the students were instructed to gather near the Lincoln Memorial at 5:40 pm to board their buses home.[7]

The basic interpretation in the mainstream media produced headlines automatically accusatory of the teens and sacralizing the Native American Omaha tribe elder and Marine veteran. Examples were: "Students in MAGA Hats Mock Native American After Rally"[8] and "Video of Boys Mocking Native American Vet, Unchecked by Adults, Sparks Uproar."[9] The media stories implied that the youth, students from Covington Catholic High School, an all-boys private school in Covington, Kentucky, were "standing extremely close to Nathan Phillips," a 64-year old Native American rights activists attending the Indigenous Peoples' March, and "were chanting, laughing and jeering."[10] All the mainstream media stories generalized the incident as a manifestation of racism in US society.

Before any investigation had taken place, the Catholic Diocese of Covington, Kentucky, issued a swift statement apologizing publicly on the boys' behalf, stating, "This behavior is opposed to the Church's teachings on the dignity and respect of the human person."[11] Politicians seized upon the assumptions made by the media. New Mexico representative Debbie Howland, now secretary of the interior, posted on Twitter that the students had been blatantly intolerant and disrespectful of a veteran and blamed the Trump administration. Martin Luther King's youngest posted a tweet that on MLK day some sort of educational action should take place. Others posted the phone numbers for Covington Catholic High School and the Church-related offices. The school took their phone number offline, Twitter users doxed the principal. Others exhorted the Twitterverse to contact the Covington Catholic diocese and even the Pope himself.[12]

The incident also became a microcosm of the perceptions surrounding the nation's polarized racial relations. The *Indigenous Peoples Movement*—which organized the Indigenous Peoples' March—stated that the actions they viewed in the video were "emblematic of our discourse in Trump's America and clearly demonstrates the validity of our concerns about the marginalization and disrespect of Indigenous peoples."[13] The Mayor of Covington, Kentucky, Joe Meyers also chimed in, writing a biting op-ed that was highly condemnatory of the students, claiming that what he saw in the video was "rightfully inspiring a tidal wave of condemnation and did NOT (sic) represent the core beliefs and values of this City."[14] The mayor essentially blamed the students without any evidence of wrongdoing other than the highly politically charged MAGA hats.

The attacks on the students were so vicious that according to Sandmann, he was receiving death threats for over a year.[15] Some celebrities and well-known commentators on Twitter tweeted their desire to see the students maimed or dead. One tweeted that he would like to smash the young man's face. He kept the video on Twitter for over a year until the threat of a lawsuit caused him to take it down.[16] *Vulture* news media reporter Erik Abriss was fired from his position stating he wanted the people in the video to die.[17]

Reporters from *NPR News* and *CNN* interviewed Nathan Phillips, whom the day after the incident embarked upon a frenzied media tour. Phillips spoke to the media as if this incident was his moment to strongly advocate for his people against racism. He implied that hundreds of teenagers were about to attack four African Americans with whom they were engaged in verbal barbs. Phillips stated his intention with walking up to the students and drumming in extremely close proximity to them was to calm the students down so they would not attack the four African American men:[18]

> tensions increased between the students—whose numbers grew from about six to an "ugly, ugly mob" of around 100 to 200—and the other protestors. "It just needed that little spark and that mob would have descended on those four guys and ripped them apart—that's what it looked like, that's what it felt like," Phillips said as he explained why he chose to walk up to the students.[19]

Phillips was very vague about the types of discussions he allegedly heard between the students and the African American men, except that in one interview he stated they were "saying their piece" (Sidner 2019) and in another he stated they were "using harsh tones" (Brookbank, Covington Catholic 2019) but never specifically quoted anyone except to state that the boys were chanting "build that wall!" In both videos, Phillips claimed he believed the students were about to attack the African Americans:

> These folks came there, these other folks were saying their piece, and these others they got offended with it . . . some of it was educational, and it was truth, and it was history about religious views and ideologies. But these young students, they couldn't see it. . . .[20]

As Phillips told it, the African Americans were offering their version of history and the students were forcefully opposing them. Other Native Americans claiming to be on the scene reported the students were chanting "Make America Great" and doing "the haka," a Maori dance, and tomahawk chops, which were disrespectful and mocking of Native American culture but regular fare in these students' sports and pep rallies.[21]

For their part, the media, wishing to showcase stories about racism and diversity, used highly leading language in their interviews with Phillips (Greene 2019).[22] *NPR* reporter David Greene, the host of "Morning Edition," prefaced his questions to Phillips as follows:

Greene: Are you saying that based on a lot of what has happened in our country recently, you were under the impression or making an assumption that a large group of young, white men might threaten a minority, who you saw, and that you saw this group of black Israel - Hebrew Israelites as potentially in danger by this large group of white men, based on what you had seen in the news in our country in recent months and years?

Phillips: Yes. Thank you for that clarity because that's what it was, in my mind and in my heart - because when I seen those—those young men could have chose to not feed into those guys, those Israelite fellers. They could have chose

. . . to exit that area . . . that this wasn't something that they needed to bring their high schools into and be involved in.[23]

In addition to being vague about the exact nature of the words exchanged between the three groups, he allowed the interviewer, who was not present at the incident, to "provide clarity." Had he done so considering the longer video that turned up a day later, this characterization of events would have been far from the truth to many viewers.

All of the initial assumptions about the incident were at first gleaned from the 25-second video showing the moment of confrontation between Nathan Phillips and the students and questioning some of the Native Americans. In those 30 seconds, Phillips had already walked up to the students and stopped in front of Sandmann, who smiled at first but as the drumming persisted, he looked away and had a slight smile on his expression. Phillips lifted the drum to Sandmann's head and continued drumming.

On January 19, 2021, however, a 1:46-hour video emerged of prior and subsequent events, whose key events from the 25-second video fell somewhere in the 1:12:00 minute to 1:15:00 time frame.[24] In this video, a small group of extremely verbally hostile African Americans called Black Hebrew Israelites (BHI), a registered hate group according to the Anti-Defamation League,[25] barraged the young men with insults for nearly one hour. This second video also provided much greater temporal context to the drumming video that incited the wild imaginations of so many Twitter and *CNN* audiences and reporters. It also captured events from a further distance and different focal length, the students from Covington Catholic High gathering on the steps of the Lincoln Memorial to await their buses.

Where the media coverage had not investigated Phillips' vague claims about the African American men, the second video demonstrated that the students experienced a full hour of the most vile invective, set off primarily by their white skin and their "MAGA" caps. Phrases heard on the video included threats of violence, accusations that they had slaves, that they were infested with insects, religious slurs, that they came from incestuous families, and that they would become school shooters. At one point, some of the boys began chanting pep rally chants to drown out the vocal BHI men. One boy tried to lead the chants by taking off his shirt and doing a pep rally dance that resembles the Polynesian "Haka" warrior dance.[26]

Moreover, contrary to Phillips' initial claim, the footage did not reveal any racist language whatsoever from the Covington Catholic students toward the African American or Native American groups. Additional videos of this scene also revealed that another Native American also stood next to Sandmann's left and was arguing with another student behind him to "go back to Europe where you came from." Sandmann looked at his schoolmate and motioned with a finger across his neck for his friend to be quiet.[27]

The verbal attacks these students endured were so outlandish that even the most progressive viewership of many television outlets wrote letters to the ombudsmen of their news stations criticizing them for jumping to conclusions before the full story was known. Moreover, an extensive investigation by the diocese of Covington, Kentucky, revealed that the students had done nothing wrong, and the diocese apologized to Nick Sandmann for apologizing to the media before the facts were known.[28] Most importantly, the video revealed that Mr. Phillips approached the boys and drummed his way into a crowd of students, leading some to question who the aggressors were.

DID THE MEDIA AND NATIVE AMERICAN COMMUNITY OVERREACT?

When tourists and student groups travel to the DC capital area, dozens and dozens of souvenir stands sell political apparel, including t-shirts with photos of the current president, and during the Trump era, the reviled "MAGA" cap. This cap, readily for sale and probably coveted by high school students in town for a pro-abortion march, had already become for but not all immigrants and minorities, the symbol of xenophobia, racism, and white nationalism.

Trump made the signature red cap a staple of all his vitriolic and racist speeches. His very first speech of 2014 announcing his presidential campaign came with an onslaught of anti-immigrant hate speech. He stated of Mexican undocumented immigrants who crossed the southern border, ". . . when Mexico sends its people, they're not sending their best. . . . They're sending people that have lots of problems, they're bringing drugs, they're bringing crime, they're rapists." As usual, he ended with a deflective bandaid, stating, "And some, I assume, are good people."[29]

Sadly, Trump's worst behavior consisted of giving implied support to outspoken white supremacists who claimed to politically support him. For example, when Trump became a candidate for the 2016 presidential election, neo-Nazi leader Richard Spencer held a meeting in Whitefish, MT, in which he raised his arm in a Nazi salute and proclaimed "Hail Trump, Hail Our People, Hail Victory." He received a thunderous standing ovation and scores of "sieg heil" salutes from the entirely white male audience.[30] On August 11, 2017, hordes of white supremacists attended a "Unite the Right" rally in which they marched with tiki torches shouting, "Jews will not replace us!" The next morning, the main march in Charlottesville was one of the bloodiest since the 1960s. Thirty-two-year-old Heather Heyer was run over by a white supremacist with an automobile and died. In response, on August 15, 2017, instead of condemning the white supremacists and the rally, Trump stated, "You had some very bad people in that group, but you also had people that were very fine people, on both sides."[31] Most importantly, President Trump attempted to manipulate voting across the United States to prevent minorities from exercising their franchise and ultimately led a riot encouraging white supremacist groups to raid the US Capitol on January 6, 2022. The repercussions and ramifications of this tragedy will be studied for decades to come.

It is clear, then, that for many minorities, the specter of 100–200 young men wearing MAGA caps gathered in an area on the steps of the Supreme Court was anxiety-producing and angering. They did not know that the students were ordered to stay in that area to catch their buses home, but they did know what a MAGA hat symbolized to them. The differences in public perception were related to the racism embedded in elements of the "MAGA" crowds.

THE FIRST VIDEO LIED

Nevertheless, too many white allies of minorities who viewed the second video had second thoughts about the way the story of the Covington Catholic students was framed. This is because the first video did not provide enough spatial and temporal context to know what was truly happening. The main issue was the use of a short video, nearly equivalent to a series of photographs. As much as a photograph can capture the outlines of physical objects, photography and videography have been a form of staging since the invention of the medium. Arguments abound about whether they should be used as "art" or "fact." Henri Cartier Bresson, for example, took candid photos as a photojournalist and attempted to provide context by capturing moments he believe were germane to the events reported but that the audience wouldn't necessarily know about but for the photo shot at the "perfect" moment.[32] In the end, a photograph projects a specific intent by its producer. Photography's modernity, after all, gave the camera user a sense that manipulating the machinery and the outcome of the photographic process could produce an intentional effect.[33]

Along the same lines of photography as a staging art, nineteenth-century philosopher and photographer Walter Benjamin noted that prior to portable cameras, photos were staged in studios using elaborate costumes, background, and lighting.[34] Moreover, it is flourishing as a form of both commercialism and as a tool to reproduce commercialism emblazoned this art form as salesmanship and illusion. Benjamin, an anti-capitalist, maintained that because modern capitalism is a social formation that obscures the relationships between people, machines, and nature, no single photograph can capture or convey any of the complexity of these relations unless it is highly choreographed or staged.[35]

Although the debate about how photographs should be used by the media continues, there is consensus among most photographers that photographs are highly staged to present a specific perspective. One way to resolve this incongruity is to focus on the truth-value of a photograph, or in the case of video, a set of photographs in a specific sequence.[36] The length of the video provides temporality or "timing" and the sections of the sequence focused upon are the "frame." Goldstein, who has written on the "truth-value" of photographs, maintains that the person behind the camera chooses to capture specific frames with specific temporality to provide an intended interpretation. Thus, photos and videos are incapable of providing "truths." Rather, only presence at the scene could provide truth as experienced by those present, not an objective truth. Goldstein therefore believes that providing more photos from more angles does not help to change someone's cultural frame, which essentially is their spatial and temporal "frame."

Columnist Ian Bogost agrees with Goldstein. The additional footage seemed to do nothing but to further affirm his initial distress about the students' racism toward Nathan Phillips. He explained in *The Atlantic* the way video is "selected, edited and re-presented has an enormous impact on the way they are received and understood."[37] He believes that neither the short nor long video depict what truly happened but offer cannon fodder for the canvas of our biased mindsets. For him, greater context doesn't provide "truth," as personally experienced. Rather, greater context reflects the intent of the video producers. Many agree with Bogost. For example, Hollywood celebrity Mira Sorvino, whose initial tweets criticized the Covington Catholic students, tweeted after the release of the longer video that the Covington Catholic boys were still at fault.

Compounding the refusal of some corners of the Twittersphere to change their perspective in response to the longer video, and to inoculate others from its impact, a meme was circulated on Twitter called #InTheLongerVideo that mocked the "facts" and the boys. As Goldstein had posited, no amount of additional "angles" or "context" could convince them that the students were anything but vile racists and manifestations of white supremacy. Attempts to prove otherwise would be automatically assumed to be a big lie.

But over the course of 1–2 weeks after the introduction of the longer video, the added context caused many in the media and the Twittersphere to retreat from their initial condemnations. Calling herself a "dolt," journalist and media expert Kara Swisher apologized for her early tweets which stated the students were "Nazi Youth."[38]

For most, the videotape had the effect of projecting each person's world views and biases onto the situation, much like a Rorschach inkblot test. Each person uses their own imagination to discern what they believe they are seeing. Political progressives who disliked President Trump and were pro-choice saw the video as a sea of young, white, privileged males against a lone, frail-looking Native American entranced in his drumming and chanting. The fact that the young men were extremely boisterous and Phillips was so frail and focused as he drummed in Sandmann's face begged this interpretation and raised the topic of race and racialization.

But perhaps the new footage of the African American hate group was so shocking for the average white suburban parent that many began to think about how their own children might react in an environment that is highly politically charged, out of their usual milieu, and lacking parental guidance (Harvey 2019).[39] Although the media should absolutely have been held accountable for not doing the type of fact checking traditional media are expected to do, such as, for example, finding out exactly what words were exchanged between the African Americans and the students, it may have been the hateful words of the Black Hebrew Israelite group that shook the average parent into giving the students some benefit of the doubt.

As it turned out, the media were also sued by Sandmann's parents for targeting and defaming a minor. The fact that Nick Sandmann was still a minor worked greatly in his favor, as children have rights to protections that adults do not. *CNN*, the network that first targeted and defamed Sandmann before investigating the matter, ended up settling a $275 million lawsuit with Sandmann's attorney on January 7, 2020; the *Washington Post* was also sued, and the legal complaint filed against them stated they had printed a long feature article full of assumptions and omissions.[40]

The complaint also derided Phillips' military service unfairly, as a

> Vietnam veteran . . . but has never been to Vietnam . . . a phony war hero . . . too intimidated by the unruly Hebrew Israelites to approach them, the true troublemakers, and instead chose to focus on a group of innocent children.[41]

Most importantly, the complaint challenged the *Washington Post* for not making more inquiries before jumping on the story, stating "The *Post* did not conduct a proper investigation before publishing its false and defamatory statements of and concerning Nicholas."[42] In the end, despite the journalistic torpor against investigating further, the *Washington Post* settled a $300 million lawsuit with the Sandmann family on July 24, 2020.[43]

Interestingly, Sandmann, whose parents could afford top attorneys to endure civil litigation against top media companies, had initially hired attorney Lin Wood, who later became embroiled in the false conspiracy to steal the 2020 elections and January 6, 2020, insurrection and attack on the US Capitol. After Wood tweeted on January 1 that Vice-President Pence "should be arrested and jailed on charges of treason and face execution by firing squad,"[44] Sandmann immediately fired him and condemned the tweet. The same day, Sandmann mentioned Wood's tweet and commented, "I'm sorry but what the hell."[45] On January 3, 2020, Wood publicly disclosed that his "plantation" in South Carolina was being used as one of the major Trump headquarters to challenge the 2020 election results.[46] But the connections between the MAGA racist establishment and Nick Sandmann's parents were also too close for comfort, and some of the Trump-wary public could ultimately not be convinced that the Covington Catholic boys were innocent.

The Covington Catholic School students came face to face with a confluence of social status and racial and historic clashes that even the most mature group of tourists could not have handled well. Although many believe that copious video footage and reams of still photos are able to add more context and exonerate the students, to know what truly happened, you had to be there.

NOTES

1. Cowicide, "Guy with a MAGA Hat Mocking a Elder Native American Protestor at Indigenous Peoples," YouTube, March 19, 2019. Accessed July 21, 2021. https://www.youtube.com/watch?v=5FogNIr2x40.

2. Beam, Adam, and Brian Melley, "Teens in 'MAGA' hats mock Native American," *Daily Hampshire Gazette,* January 20, 2019.

3. Bekiempis, Victoria, "Covington Catholic High Apologizes for Students Who Mocked Native American Veteran During March for Life," *The Daily Beast,* March 20, 2019.

4. Hassert, Dan, "Mayor Meyer: Covington 'appalled,'" *Covington Government,* January 19, 2019.

5. Taitano, Kaya, "Differing Narratives After Standoff Between Native American Man, High School Student," *NPR.ORG,* January 21, 2019.

6. Greene, David, "Outcry Results After Video Appears to Show Students Mocking Native American Man," Morning Edition, *NPR News,* January 21, 2019.

7. Brookbank, Sarah, "Analysis: What the Video from the Incident at the Indigenous Peoples March Tell Us about What Happened," *Cincinnati Enquirer,* January 20, 2019.

8. Greene, "Outcry Results After Video Appears to Show Students Mocking Native American Man."

9. Ujifusa, Andrew, "Video of Boys Mocking Native American Vet, Unchecked by Adults, Sparks Uproar," *Education Week.* January 19, 2019.

10. Greene, "Outcry Results After Video Appears to Show Students Mocking Native American Man."

11. Associated Press, "Covington Catholic HS Students Were Not Instigators in Confrontational Video, Kentucky Bishop Says," *ABC11 Raleigh-Durham*, 20 February 2019.

12. Tchaz, "Here's an idea, direct your anger and the schools contact information (as I just did) to POPE FRANCIS @Pontifex Covington Catholic High School:

Principal Robert Rowe: browe@covcath.org phone: (859) 491-2247 Diocese of Covington: Phone: 859-392-1500," January 19, 2019, 4:27pm, Tweet.

13. Pasquini, Maria, "Native American Veteran Says He Tried to Keep Peace as MAGA-Hat-Wearing Teens Harassed Him," *PEOPLE.com,* 2019. Accessed July 13, 2020. https://people.com/politics/maga-hat-wearing-teenagers-harass-native-american-veteran/.

14. Hassert, Dan, "Mayor Meyer: Covington 'appalled,'" *Covington Government.* January 19, 2019.

15. London, Matt, "'Covington Kid' Nick Sandmann Says He's Lived Under 'Constant Threat' for over a Year," *FoxNews.Com.* April 13, 2020.

16. Richardson, Valerie, "Ex-CNN Host 'Likely' to be Sued over Now-Deleted 'Punchable Face' Tweet: Sandmann Attorney," *Washington Times,* January 13, 2020.

17. Stieber, Zachary, 2019, "Archdiocese Apologizes for Hasty Statement About Covington Students," *NTD News.* January 24, 2019.

18. Brookbank, "Analysis: What the Video from the Incident at the Indigenous Peoples March Tell Us about What Happened."

19. Sidner, Sarah, "Native American Elder Nathan Phillips, in His Own Words," *Central News Network (CNN),* January 21, 2019.

20. Sidner, "Native American Elder Nathan Phillips, in His Own Words."

21. Beam, Adam, and Brian Melley, "Teens in 'MAGA' Hats Mock Native American," *Daily Hampshire Gazette*, January 20, 2019.

22. Greene, "Outcry Results After Video Appears to Show Students Mocking Native American Man."

23. Greene, "Outcry Results After Video Appears to Show Students Mocking Native American Man.

24. Reaction, "FULL 1h30 Video: Covington Catholic Students MAGA Hat Kids vs Nathan Phillips," *YouTube*, January 19, 2019.

25. Anti-Defamation League Staff, 2018, "Two Years Ago, They Marched in Charlottesville. Where Are They Now?" *Anti-Defamation League,* accessed June 10, 2022. https://www.adl.org/resources/blog/two-years-ago-they-marched-charlottesville-where-are-they-now.

26. Brookbank, "Analysis: What the Video from the Incident at the Indigenous Peoples March Tell Us about What Happened."

27. Brookbank, "Analysis: What the Video from the Incident at the Indigenous Peoples March Tell Us about What Happened."

28. Romero, Dennis, 2019. "Covington Bishop Apologizes to Teen in Face-off with Native American," *NBC News*, January 25, 2019.

29. Scott, Eugene, "Trump's Most Insulting—and Violent—Language Is Often Reserved for Immigrants," *Washington Post,* October 2, 2019.

30. The Atlantic YouTube Channel, "'Hail Trump!': Richard Spencer Speech Excerpts," *YouTube.Com*, November 21, 2016. Accessed June 10, 2022. https://www.youtube.com/watch?v=1o6-bi3jlxk.

31. Kessler, Glenn, "The 'Very Fine People' at Charlottesville: Who Were They?" *The Washington Post*, May 8, 2020.

32. Chan, Lauren. 2019. "Henri Cartier-Bresson and the Value of Photography," *The Cambridge Student,* January 30, 2019. Accessed May 20, 2021. https://www.tcs.cam.ac.uk/henri-cartier-bresson-and-the-value-of-photography/.

33. Sontag, Susan, *On Photography* (New York: Farrar, Straus and Giroux, 1977).

34. Leslie, Esther, "Walter Benjamin and the Birth of Photography." In *On Photography,* edited by Esther Leslie (London: Reaktion Books, 2015).

35. Leslie, "Walter Benjamin and the Birth of Photography."

36. Goldstein, Barry M., "All Photos Lie: Images as Data." In *Visual Research Methods: Image, Society, and Representation*, edited by Gregory C. Stanczak (Thousand Oaks: SAGE Publications, 2007).

37. Bogost, Ian, "Stop Trusting Viral Videos," *The Atlantic,* January 22, 2019, p. 2.

38. Flanagan, Caitlin, "The Media Botched the Covington Catholic Story," *The Atlantic,* January 25, 2019.

39. Harvey, Jennifer, "Enough Finger-Pointing: That Kid in the MAGA Hat Is My Kid! (He's Yours, Too)," *Yes Magazine,* January 28, 2019.

40. Quinn, Liam, "Nick Sandmann's Attorney Reveals Lawsuit Against CNN," *Australian News Service,* March 10, 2019.

41. Sandmann et al. v. Cable News Network, No. 2:19-cv-00031-DLB-CJS. 12 March 2019. Accessed July 20, 2022. https://www.documentcloud.org/documents/5769734-Sandmann-v-Cnn.

42. Farhi, Paul, "The Washington Post Sued by Family of Covington Catholic Teenager," *Washington Post,* February 19, 2019.

43. KKTV News Staff, "CNN Settles Lawsuit with Covington Catholic Student Involved in Protest," *KKTV News,* June 7, 2020.

44. Grasha, Kevin, "'This Is a Dumb Tweet': Nick Sandmann Fires Attorney Lin Wood after Twitter, Telegram Posts," *Cincinnati Enquirer*, January 26, 2021.

45. Grasha, "'This Is a Dumb Tweet.'"

46. Schwartz, Brian, "Pro-Trump Lawyer Says His Plantations Were Go-to Spots for Those Aiming to Overturn the 2020 Election."

Chapter 4

No Sense of Face

This chapter focuses on the story of an intelligent man who was so greatly deceived by an online predator that his life was destroyed. Examining this tragedy, I seek to explore with the audience how he could have been so thoroughly deceived by someone he had never met but communicated with several times a day. More importantly, I use the case study to determine how much social media users who are predators can hide about themselves on electronic media, and how the technology itself mediates the fraud. To make sense of the tragedy, I employ the work of Erving Goffman to examine how and why the victim was unable to perceive any inconsistencies or red flags in the perpetrator's online behavior.

In Goffman's theory of the presentation of self, users create impressions in their profiles that represent the self they wish to put forward to their audiences. Profiles, including personal and business profiles, are used to portray a specific credible impression to users, and followers, to the exclusion of other impressions. Erving Goffman[1] had described this process as "impression management," defining it as "accentuating some aspects of behavior that increase credibility in favor of those that might discredit the fostered impression."[2] Goffman opens with a sentence that states the necessity of a physical presence of two people before impression management becomes possible: "when an individual enters the presence of others, they commonly seek to acquire information about him or to bring into play information about him already possessed."[3] To accomplish impression management virtually, or online, users must curate a profile that represents a persona or representation of a person that may or may not be true, using meaningful posts, staging photos and posting articles or memes that signal their interests and concerns to their followers, and portray a positive persona.

For Goffman, the interaction between two or more people in the physical world resembles a play. Actors put on a facade relevant to the person they are interacting with. The facade is labeled by Goffman as the "frontstage." The goal is to make the best impression of oneself while hiding facts and factors that give contrary impressions. Goffman calls the hidden areas that would cast doubt on the facade the "backstage."[4]

For the "frontstage," Goffman defines it as "furniture and other background items which supply the scenery and stage props for the spate of human action played out before, within, or upon it."[5] He is not specific about a location when describing the backstage, defining it as "a place relative to a given performance, where the impression fostered by the performance is knowingly contradicted as a matter of course."[6] Most importantly, backstage is a place where not only does the actor expect explicitly not to be in contact with the audience but also the place they use to construct the frontstage facade. Lastly, backstage is also the place where the actor can "relax and step out of character."[7]

Goffman gave as an example of backstage, a quote from French philosopher Simon de Bouvoir's seminal volume *The Second Sex*. She described women's frontstage behavior when they are with men, versus their backstage behavior when in the company of other women: "When with her husband . . . every woman is more or less conscious of the thought, 'I am not myself.'. . . With other women, a woman . . . is polishing her equipment but not in battle."[8]

Other examples that Goffman gave of backstage were the front and back of an auto mechanic workshop, a mortuary, and a hotel kitchen, where backstage was carefully hidden from the customers, to conceal the realities of preparing and providing a final product in the polished front stage and a busy, cacophonous backstage. These were all examples of physical locations with physical audiences or customers.

One wonders the utility of Goffman with applications to social and other electronic media but needn't wonder too long. Scores of papers from various fields have used Goffman to describe the presentation of self on radio, television, and more recently social media.[9,10,11,12,13,14,15,16,17,18]

Without alluding to the spatial disruption of frontstage and backstage caused by media, Goffman himself gave a prescient example. He stated that announcers in radio and television broadcasting studios have a backstage defined as "all places out of range of the cameras and the live microphones."[19] He added that an announcer holding a sponsor's product—which he clearly does not like—at arm's length, while holding his nose out of the field of view of the camera, is an example of frontstage and backstage involving electronic media. The product in his hand and his broadcast words were the frontstage, but the holding of his nose out of view of the camera was the backstage.

This example was the first distinctive media example of how electronic media disrupts space, including frontstage and backstage, from physical spaces to more discursive spatial arrangements that change quickly and are subject to accidental revelation. Goffman knew the precarity of staging on media, stating that for broadcasters, "backstage" was "very treacherous" because the chance of getting before a hot mic or a live camera was relatively high.[20] It can be assumed, therefore, that "backstage" on the internet is also a matter of what is hidden from audiences and frontstage is what the audiences are privy to. Frontstage, then, can be what users choose to reveal in their profiles, and backstage can seep through if potential deceivers respond incongruently to others in their private or public chats, or if their activity in other online spaces is accidentally revealed by the platform or internet provider to be contrary to what the user themself present to their social media followers.

One groundbreaking scholar who early on in the digital revolution realized the spatial disruption brought on by electronic media was John Meyrowitz, who theorized the phenomenon in *No Sense of Place*.[21] Using television as an example, Meyrowitz stated that the ubiquity of messaging and stories from around the world coming into peoples' homes reveals new information to viewers that they otherwise would not be privy to. Meyrowitz gave numerous examples of how controlling and screening behaviors by, for example, separating audiences are extremely difficult as a result of electronic media. TV messaging about vast varieties of peoples and situations, beamed into the homes of viewers, has made notions of hierarchy and social roles obsolete and disassembled the "situational geography" of social life.

Electronic media, in Meyrowitz's view, had made the projection of our various "selves" to different, separate audiences nearly impossible and undermined the importance or significance of "place." He stated that people "no longer have a place matched to a physical location and audiences found in them."[22] Hence, all electronic media has rendered the people of the world with "no sense of place." Today, social media profiles and their potential to hide the backstage gives us "no sense of face".

Goffman wrote in 1953, the heyday of American postwar television, which was broadcast in format. Audiences received programming in their homes and offices but did not have an opportunity to produce content or to give feedback in real time to their television studio or other viewers. The separation between frontstage and backstage may have been blurred, but audiences did not have opportunities to communicate with one another, and the separation between producer and audience was absolute. For most of the 20th century, in fact, it was difficult to realize the disruptive potential of media when it was so difficult for audiences to give content producers or one another instant input. Television and radio communications necessitated the use of sophisticated and expensive equipment and expertise that only a few well-organized broadcasting companies could provide.

When audiences also became content producers after the digital media revolution, not only were front and backstage disrupted, but society blurred the lines between "the show" and "the audience," and even fantasy and reality. Fantasy life online and reality at home became commonplace. Others spoke of their true cares and vulnerabilities with strangers online, while ignoring their families at home.

By 1986, the time of Meyrowitz's research, advances in miniaturization, video compression, and the analog-to-digital transition of the late 20th century enabled a greater proportion of the public to produce and transmit their own content using light equipment and technology. Over the past 25 years, the revolution in digital communications technology has in fact, created a veritable explosion of content. But much of the conversations and content on social media can be deceptive.

The upshot of this creative explosion is a treacherous environment in which users have some ability to control their profile presentation and hide their backstage, but also encounter many disruptive factors that can reveal their backstage depending on the platform's algorithms and depending on the curiosity and zeal of those the user is interacting with. Facebook and Twitter, for example, use algorithms that, although somewhat customizable, make it greatly difficult to know which "friends" or followers can see which posts. Chances for social errors with mixed audiences remain high. Moreover, many platforms constantly change user controls for privacy and security, the very controls that enable users to control their backstage and keep it out of specific audiences' view.

Today, social media users have varied motivations for creating a specific profile or brand, and the images they wish to convey are also varied.[23,24,25,26,27,28] Some merely curate happy moments for friends and family, others present a credible professional persona to potential customers, and a minority of bad actors create false profiles to scam unwitting targets out of money. For example, in the case of travel selfies, friends who know the profile creator in physical life have a realistic idea of how different from "reality" the profile creator's life happens to be. But an online dating situation between strangers who have deceptive profiles could lead to suspicion and bad feelings when the truth is discovered.

The typical profile of curating happy moments consists of presenting photos to friends and archiving days, months, and years of photos of memorable moments. These may include work conferences, day trips, and other travel selfies. Over time, their profile reveals the newsfeed of a life that is lacking the banal. For those posting mostly positive memories, their profiles enable them and their friends to maintain a healthy outlook on life by only publicly sharing and revisiting the positive. Posting festive pictures may also be a way to gain positive self-esteem by receiving as many likes and follows from their friends and family as possible. Many profile creators gain salutary feelings from sharing good times with friends who cannot be there in person.

There are those who are more narcissistic and curate posts to give the impression that they are always doing something glamorous, seeking to keep their audience's attention, and to gain approval through as many likes and follows as possible. Many strive to reach the maximum number of followers.[29,30] Others nearly exclusively snapshot selfies, often at glamorous resorts or other expensive facilities, wearing designer clothing, staged with celebrities, models, or other highly attractive persons.

There are also cases where the cost of the egregious difference in frontstage and backstage behavior occurs with fictitious profiles created by fraudsters and con artists. These profiles are created to lure victims for financial and/or emotional gain and usually feature pseudonyms and stolen identities, stolen photos, and other false information posted solely to cause immense harm through con artistry for emotional and/or material gain.

Sometimes the con games take place entirely online. At other times they extend to the telephone. Rarely, however, do these fraudsters conduct physical encounters. As per Goffman's theory, physical presence greatly increases the chances of the backstage leaking through to the prospective victims. Social media platforms have greatly increased the ability of criminals to succeed in fraud by easing the ability to harvest potential victims and promoting the ability to remain anonymous by hiding behind a profile page on social media.

CASE STUDY OF PROFILE DECEPTION: THE TRAGEDY OF PROFESSOR JAMES AUNE

One of the stories I explore—because of the extremes in both the methods and the results of fraud, or hiding one's face, and the vast difference between a profile and physical reality—is the tragic story of Professor James Aune, a professor of communications at Texas A&M University (TAMU) in College Station, Texas, who in 2013 fell victim to a sex scam that resulted in his suicide. Aune committed suicide because he believed his online sexual exploits were about to be revealed to friends, family, and the academic community.[31,32] In fact, none of the people Aune believed he was communicating with were real people. They were the artifact of a fraudster's sordid imagination. The anonymity provided by social media combined with the ability of Aune's fraudster to target him based on specific characteristics and the social media chat rooms Aune selected led to his ultimate demise.

James Aune had been in a long-term marriage with his wife, Miriam, also a professor of communications, and had two nonverbal autistic young adult sons named Nick and Don. Miriam relinquished her position at TAMU to care for their sons. According to his colleagues and wife, Aune had always been an avid consumer of technology and became an avid blogger. Miriam stated in a documentary investigation on Discovery Channel that Aune used blogging and other online activity an outlet to vent his feelings and engage in social life with community members whom he separated from his friends and family. Professor Paul Stob, a close friend of Aune, admitted that blogging was an emotional and intellectual outlet for Aune.[33]

At first, Aune began blogging on the Rhetorical Society of America's Blogora, a metaphorical agora or a marketplace of ideas. This blog enabled Aune to become a little more personal with other rhetoricians who understood his cultural and academic references. As Aune approached his mid-50s, he also began to explore his sexuality by visiting gay and transgender social media chat rooms. Chat rooms late at night in his university office gave Aune a sense of being protected and concealed while still engaging in intrigue with multiple, unknown others. Aune antiseptically separated his online sex life from his physical life, that is, his friends and colleagues, and his family. However, he did not separate facts about his real life from strangers he was communicating with online. His intimate communication with strangers, and his failure to realize that their profile is a scant representation of what someone with much to hide, ultimately led to his undoing.

Gradually, the separation between Aune's online life and his family, friends, and colleagues became greater. Professor Stob stated that Aune became increasingly selective about what he shared with whom, indicating that he was deeply engaged in prophylactic impression management and had a tremendous amount of collateral that he concealed from his friends and family. Above all, he prized maintaining his prestige in a community of scholars as a respectable, intellectual, and associate professor at a major university. He also believed that activities he maintained online would never affect his physical life or reputation.

Aune eventually engaged in adventuresome and risqué sexual encounters that began online and on at least one occasion led to a gay casual sex encounter in 2008, five years prior to his suicide.[34] On that occasion, Aune had told his wife that he was traveling to UT Austin to use their library and immediately upon his return admitted to her that he had in fact engaged in a sexual encounter with a male stranger he had met online.[35] After a few weeks of feeling contrite, Aune again began online intrigue in gay and transgender chatrooms. One persona he created was called "Texas Top," indicating his sexual preference as the active person in gay sex.

Aune soon began an online relationship, initially using the pseudonym "Texas Top" on a transgender digital platform, and then moving to text messages. His love interest was a young transgender woman named Karen, who claimed she was 19 years old. On the platform, they exchanged increasing numbers of messages, and eventually exchanged their cell phone numbers so they could send photos and texts. Karen had all the marks of a vulnerable and fearful young person who sought the emotional and intellectual support of an older established and prestigious man. She often praised his appearance and flattered him as a young woman in love with an older man. This caused Aune to feel flattered and to reveal much information about his real life to Karen.

After some weeks of exchanging amorous and risqué text messages, Karen revealed that she was not 19, but 16 years of age. Aune was so intrigued by Karen that he nevertheless continued the online relationship despite the grave legal danger of soliciting sex with a minor. Their relationship deepened and soon Karen and Aune began exchanging sexual conversation and eventually nude photographs.

A few weeks into the intrigue, his cell phone rang and an angry man claiming to be Karen's father demanded he cease his online exploits with his daughter Karen, or he would alert the police and his friends and university. Aune was alarmed and eventually told his wife and hired an attorney. Karen's father's threats continued, eventually including the demand for money to send a traumatized Karen into therapy. The father demanded $5,000, which Aune was only able to provide a fraction of, by raiding his meager savings. Home care of their autistic sons cost them large sums, and they lived frugally.[36] Suddenly, activities that were "backstage" to his real, physical life seeped hopelessly through and threatened to doom his marriage, career, and liberty.

Attempting to restore his life before the online and legal troubles, Aune decided to take a leave of absence from the university to solve his personal and legal issues. On the day he went to the office to clear out his belongings, his staff informed him that they had received calls from a man who stated that Aune had sexually exploited a student. Moreover, Karen's father had also left an accusatory remark on a website on which students rated professors, suggesting in his comments on the site that Aune had "taught Karen a lot." Suddenly, Aune believed that his academic persona would be marred by Karen's father's revelations.[37]

The father's angry demands for money intensified, and Karen's father had come through with his threats to reveal his transgressions to people in his "real world." That morning, a series of text messages fired via Karen's phone by his blackmailer, Karen's father, ended with a panicked Aune texting "I am going to kill myself and you will go to prison for blackmail." Minutes later, Aune drove up to the TAMU north campus parking lot, walked up to the ledge, and hurled himself to his death.[38]

The police and FBI soon discovered that Aune's blackmailer was a middle-aged man named Daniel Duplaisir.[39] He had created Karen's persona using explicit photos of his own daughter whom he had sexually molested in the past and for which he had been convicted of child sex abuse.[40,41,42] In the words of a law enforcement specialist working on the case, “there had been no Karen” and “there had been no Karen’s father.”[43]

These were two false personae that were a product of Duplaisir’s imagination. Yet the online anonymity provided by social media and chatroom technology enabled Duplaisir to impersonate a nonexistent transgender teenager and fool Aune into a relationship that for him was very real. The fact that Duplaisir had a daughter whom he had taken explicit photos of as a teenager gave him great familiarity with young, exploited girls. He was likely also intimately familiar with pornography and transgender dating sites. This enabled him to present an authentic facade while he was courting his mark. In addition, the real photos of his daughter used in the scam also added to the deception against Aune. The genuine photos gave Aune the idea that he was indeed communicating with the person whose photos he was observing. Duplaisir’s familiarity with his own daughter caused Aune to fail to realize that, despite weeks of communication, he was speaking to a middle-aged man who had no interest whatsoever in Aune but to entrap and extort him. These familiarities enabled Duplaisir to put on a plausible appearance on both the transgender website and the text messaging.

The tragedy brings home the idea that without adequate media literacy about the potential for fraud on social media even the most intelligent people unexpectedly find a world of trouble online. For sites that carry on the activity that is socially shunned, such as pornography sites and online dating sites, users must be aware of the grave risks involved in not knowing the realities behind the false profiles. In addition, future efforts at media literacy should concentrate on educating users to ask the right questions and exercise caution about revealing too much backstage information when they meet someone online. Last, social media platforms must standardize privacy controls so that consumers have consistent control over how much information they wish to reveal to audiences.

NOTES

1. Goffman, Erving, *The Presentation of Self in Everyday Life* (New York: Anchor Books/Doubleday, 1959).
2. Goffman, *The Presentation of Self in Everyday Life*, 14.
3. Goffman, *The Presentation of Self in Everyday Life*, 2.
4. Goffman, *The Presentation of Self in Everyday Life*, 119.
5. Goffman, *The Presentation of Self in Everyday Life*, 22.
6. Goffman, *The Presentation of Self in Everyday Life*, 112.
7. Goffman, *The Presentation of Self in Everyday Life*, 112.

8. Goffman, Erving, *The Presentation of Self in Everyday Life*, 113.

9. Bullingham, Liam, and Ana C. Vasconcelos, "'The Presentation of Self in the Online World': Goffman and the Study of Online Identities," *Journal of Information Science* 39: 101–112.

10. Fox, Jesse, and Margaret C. Rooney, "The Dark Triad and Trait Self-Objectification as Predictors of Men's Use and Self-Presentation Behaviors on Social Networking Sites," *Personality and Individual Differences* 76 (2015): 161–165.

11. Hogan, Bernie, "The Presentation of Self in the Age of Social Media: Distinguishing Performances and Exhibitions Online," *Bulletin of Science, Technology & Society* 30 (2010): 377–386.

12. Hollenbaugh, Erin E., "Self-Presentation in Social Media: Review and Research Opportunities," *Review of Communication Research* 9 (2021): 80–98.

13. Lee-Won, Roselyn J., Minsun Shim, Yeon Kyoung Joo, and Sung Gwan Park, "Who Puts the Best 'Face' Forward on Facebook?: Positive Self-Presentation in Online Social Networking and the Role of Self-Consciousness, Actual-to-Total Friends Ratio, and Culture," *Computers in Human Behavior* 39 (2014): 413–423.

14. Lyu, Seong Ok, "Travel Selfies on Social Media as Objectified Self-Presentation," *Tourism Management (1982)* 54 (2016): 185–195.

15. Merunkova, Lucie, and Josef Slerka, "Goffman's Theory as a Framework for Analysis of Self Presentation on Online Social Networks," *Masaryk University Journal of Law and Technology* 13 (2019): 243–276.

16. Ross, Drew A. R., "Backstage with the Knowledge Boys and Girls: Goffman and Distributed Agency in an Organic Online Community," *Organization Studies* 28 (2007): 307–325.

17. Schwarz, Kaylan C., "'Gazing' and 'Performing': Travel Photography and Online Self-Presentation," *Tourist Studies* 21 (2021): 260–277.

18. Trysnes, Irene, and Ronald Mayora Synnes, "The Role of Religion in Young Muslims' and Christians' Self-Presentation on Social Media," *YOUNG* 30 (2022): 281–296.

19. Goffman, *The Presentation of Self in Everyday Life*, 119.

20. Goffman, *The Presentation of Self in Everyday Life*.

21. Meyrowitz, J., *No Sense of Place: The Impact of Electronic Media on Social Behavior* (New York: Oxford University Press, 1986).

22. Meyrowitz, *No Sense of Place*, 7.

23. Carpenter, Christopher J., "Narcissism on Facebook: Self-Promotional and Anti-Social Behavior," *Personality and Individual Differences* 52, no. 4 (2012): 482–486.

24. AARP, "Fake Dating Profiles Used to Lure Women in Dating Scam," *AARP.ORG,* August 23, 2019.

25. Khoshsabk, Nastaran, and Jane Southcott, "Gender Identity and Facebook: Social Conservatism and Saving Face," *The Qualitative Report; Fort Lauderdale* 24 (2019): 632–647.

26. Daniels, Elizabeth A., "Sexiness on Social Media: The Social Costs of Using a Sexy Profile Photo," *Sexualization, Media, & Society* (December 2016).

27. Schauer, Frederick F., *Profiles, Probabilities, and Stereotypes* (London: Harvard University Press, 2009).

28. Tufekci, Zeynep, "Can You See Me Now? Audience and Disclosure Regulation in Online Social Network Sites," *Bulletin of Science, Technology & Society* 28 (2008): 20–36.

29. Carpenter, "Narcissism on Facebook," 482–486.

30. Bergman, Shawn M., Matthew E. Fearrington, Shaun W. Davenport, and Jacqueline Z. Bergman, "Millennials, Narcissism, and Social Networking: What Narcissists Do on Social Networking Sites and Why," *Personality and Individual Differences* 50 (2011): 706–711.

31. Fisher, Jim, "Professor James Aune Chose Death over Disgrace," *Jim Fisher True Crime Blog,* March 2013. Accessed June 13, 2020. https://jimfishertruecrime.blogspot.com/2013/03/professor-james-aune-chose-death-over.html.

32. Clifton, Dan, "Web of Lies: Online Education," Television Production, directed by Dan Clifton, produced by Ellen Arnold, *Investigation Discovery,* Accessed July 10, 2021. https://www.investigationdiscovery.com/tv-shows/web-of-lies/full-episodes/online-education, https://www.investigationdiscovery.com/tv-shows/web-of-lies/full-episodes/online-education?code=024f12320af46381389cb3463913d4f2efff3be4&state=nonce%2CrqQVVqUYfJZ8OQVLvPLyjI0jJ6s7eK0E.

33. Clifton, "Web of Lies: Online Education."

34. Clifton, "Web of Lies: Online Education."

35. Clifton, "Web of Lies: Online Education."

36. Clifton, "Web of Lies: Online Education."

37. Clifton, "Web of Lies: Online Education."

38. Clifton, "Web of Lies: Online Education."

39. Lozano, Juan A., "Dad Denies Using Daughter in Child-Porn Extortion Plot after Professor's Suicide," *NBC News Online,* March 27, 2013.

40. Lozano, "Dad Denies Using Daughter in Child-Porn Extortion Plot after Professor's Suicide."

41. Schiller, Dane, "Alleged Blackmail Behind A&M Professor's Suicide," *Houston Chronicle,* March 25, 2013.

42. Dubois, Ross, "The Strange and Sordid End of an A&M Professor," *Texas Monthly,* March 27, 2013.

43. Clifton, "Web of Lies: Online Education."

Chapter 5

News Worlds

What is news? What is fact? Why do we depend on it? And how do social media actors affect, frame, and distort what we know? In today's fast-changing information landscape, the nature of news and of "facts" themselves is being reoriented and reconstructed. This includes the conventions in the recognition and distribution of narratives across social groups. Activists with agendas, journalists with ideas about what constitutes a news story, and changes in how these activities are bankrolled all have an influence.

With the advent of the internet, mobile computing, and information technology databases, we now live in a world of *virtual* news and *virtual* facts. Of course, disputes over facts are as old as humankind. Hence there are layers upon layers of courts and legal processes. But in the digital era and its hordes of professional and amateur journalists, it is left to each member of the public to discern what is true and what is important both personally and to society.

With thousands, if not millions of new online "news" sites portraying their reporting as journalism, it is hard for even the most sophisticated news consumer to know what to believe. News and fact verification has indeed become so complex that consumers must resort to truth verification sites, like FactCheck.org, Snopes, Media Bias/Fact Check, and ThoughtCo., to ferret out the facts and assess the bias and credibility of "virtual news."

Two new entrants in the digital news ecosystem are indeed drastically redefining the mass information landscape: (1) partisan online "news" media outlets and (2) the participation of news consumers on conventional mass media website portals.

VERITAS AUT FICTIO?

Go on Media Bias/Fact Check and search for right- and left-bias outlets, and you'll find a virtual pandora's box of entrants purporting to offer the truth. Many, such as Gateway Pundit, Parler, and 4Chan on the right and Deep Left Field, are on the political extremes and have been judged to have very low factual content or credibility. But many of the new mass media sites are more subtle, with mixed factual content, just enough to stay on the radar as plausibly reliable. These are the most difficult sites to evaluate.

One of these controversial but influential news media actors is James O'Keefe, a politically conservative undercover filmmaker and the founder of *Project Veritas,* an online mass media organization that targets progressive and liberal organizations and individuals. Closely associated with Breitbart News, another extreme right outlet, O'Keefe has become a poster boy for alt-right virtual news industry journalism. O'Keefe's *modus operandi* is to shoot surreptitious videos while interacting with his targets in various disguises and staged scenarios. After the videos are shot, he selectively edits them for maximum incriminating effect and circulates them on social media and through other news outlets as *exposés*.

O'Keefe rose to national prominence in 2008, with a viral sting on Planned Parenthood. That was followed in 2009 with an *exposé* on the Association of Community Organizations for Reform Now (ACORN). These productions came out in the midst of rising conservative angst about the candidacy and eventual election of the country's first black president, and the Great Recession of 2007–2009, and resonated with that public.

Then Senator Barack Obama's 2008 presidential candidacy greatly polarized the American people, and conservatives spent much of the campaign attempting to delegitimize Obama with inuendo, including the well-publicized birther controversy that disputed he was born in the United States. His opponents also engaged in a campaign to mock Obama's former career as a "community organizer" in Chicago, Illinois. For example, during the vice-presidential debates, the Republican candidate Sarah Palin, then mayor of Wasilla, Alaska, mocked Obama's career *bona fides* stating, ". . . being a small-town mayor is sort of like a community organizer, except that you have actual responsibilities."[1]

The Great Recession, America's worst economic downturn since the Great Depression of 1929, happened on the Republicans' watch and devastated the United States and global economy. Decades-old investment firms such as Lehman Brothers and Bear Stearns went bust. Other US financial institutions had to be bailed out by the Federal Government to the tune of $778 billion.[2]

The American public was greatly divided about the causes of the recession, the justification of the bailouts, and particularly who was to blame. The recession was precipitated primarily by the collapse of a housing market bubble facilitated by greatly relaxed Federal rules for home mortgage lending. Under the rules, millions of financially marginal borrowers became first-time homeowners using easy-to-get, no- or low-down payment, initially variable-interest rate loans.

To monetize the mortgages, and hedge their risks, the mortgage banks packaged the loans into derivative investment instruments. These mortgage-backed securities were profitable and provided liquidity while the housing market was strong, and for as long as housing prices continued to rise the homebuyers could sell or refinance their homes at the end of the typically three-year terms to lock in yet another low variable interest rate loan.

But in 2006, the housing market slowed, and the less-solvent homeowners began defaulting on their then high-interest rate mortgages. Cash flow and credit suddenly seized throughout the US financial system. By late 2008, the markets had dropped 50% over 18 months.[3]

Progressives blamed predatory lending and "casino capitalists" for the Great Recession. Conservatives blamed low-income homeowners for taking out mortgages they couldn't afford but were able to get with the assistance of "homeowner assistance" groups such as *ACORN*.[4]

Founded in 1970 by George Wiley and Wade Rathke, *ACORN* was a loose network of nonpartisan 501(c)(3) nonprofit charitable groups, a national non-profit, nonstock financial organization, the *ACORN Housing Corporation*, and a nationwide umbrella organization established as a 501(c)(4) that engages in lobbying.

By 2008 *ACORN* had grown into an influential advocate for low- and moderate-income families. Between 1998 and 2008 *ACORN* helped its low- and middle-income constituents gain greater economic power through home ownership, reportedly securing $15 billion in HUD financing.[5] In addition, *ACORN*'s affiliated nonprofits trained their constituents to gain political power by becoming political candidates and sponsoring progressive ballot initiatives. And during the Great Recession, *ACORN* assisted financially stressed homeowners to prevent foreclosure.

It was against this backdrop of economic crisis and growing conservative resentment that James O'Keefe rose to prominence using miniaturized cameras and false personae to produce "gotcha" videos, including his *exposé* targeting *ACORN*. O'Keefe's work was, indeed, so wildly successful that *ACORN* was bankrupt within less than a year.[6]

For the *ACORN exposé*, O'Keefe approached *ACORN* offices with a friend, Hannah Giles, impersonating a pimp and prostitute, respectively, to compel *ACORN* staff to give them housing advice despite having been told that the couple was engaged in illegal sex work. In his debut video *exposé*, O'Keefe pulled no punches that his goal was to "destroy the enemy" *ACORN*.

O'Keefe unabashedly portrayed himself as an ardent rogue activist seeking to weed out corruption on the political left, referring to left-wing author Saul Alinsky's *Rules for Radicals*, which urges grassroots organizers to "pick the target, freeze it, personalize it, polarize it . . . identify a responsible individual . . ."[7] O'Keefe claimed his goal was to "expose the absurdities of the enemy by employing their own rules and language."[8]

One Latino worker for *ACORN* San Diego was recorded asking questions and offering information about sex trafficking across the US-Mexico border. He was summarily fired by *ACORN* when the video surfaced. The Latino worker later explained to reporter Conor Friedersdorf[9] that he tried to "go along" with the sex trafficking talk proposed by O'Keefe acting as a pimp in order to garner as much information as possible to give to law enforcement. When the Attorney General of California investigated the incident, he discovered that the worker had indeed notified his cousin, a police officer, who in turn contacted Federal human trafficking law enforcement officials. The worker had also immediately notified his *ACORN* supervisor about the incident.

Four years later, the Latino worker won a lawsuit against O'Keefe for $100,000 and Giles for $50,000 for videotaping him without his consent. But the damage to the worker's career and the injustice of being maligned as a sex trafficker still lingers. Friedersdorf also approached O'Keefe and his most ardent supporter, conservative social media pundit Andrew Breitbart, about their refusal to correct the Breitbart.com website entries about the exonerated worker. Breitbart continued for several months to insinuate falsities about the worker[10] and aided O'Keefe in raising more funds based on the falsities.

One headline about the sting appeared in the September 14, 2009, Metro section of the *New York Post* reading "Pimp and hooker catch Brooklyn staff." Numerous investigations later exonerated *ACORN* of wrongdoing, but the damage was done. All of O'Keefe's videos are doctored for maximum shock value and deception, and the *ACORN* video was no exception. Audiences saw *ACORN* counselors seemingly unconcerned about having sex workers as prospective clients and demonstrating solicitousness to a pair engaged in willful moral corruption and obvious illegality.[11,12]

O'Keefe's targeting of an organization dedicated to easing ballot access for the working class and assisting low-income Americans with housing and government benefits was central to his conservative activism. And he made clear that his goal was to destroy *ACORN*. "If you can make impossible demands on your enemy, you can destroy them," he stated to the *New York Post*.[13]

From the onset of his career, O'Keefe has sought to portray himself as a legitimate journalist dedicated to reshape what we call "news." He has described himself as the vanguard of the "new" 21st-century media featuring digital technology, and he aggressively promotes controversial reporting tactics, especially surreptitious videotaping of targets. He has stated of his techniques that "undercover, guerrilla tactics are the future of investigative journalism and political activism."[14]

Recently *Project Veritas*, apparently flush in funding, has embarked on a major expansion. On their website they now are seeking investigative journalists who do not need a degree or writing sample but do need to have a "hunter's mentality," a "track record of successfully challenging the status quo," and "a distrust of both public and private institutions and people in positions of power who want to be the first to that bombshell story on your platforms."[15] These are not the *bona fides* of the most skilled journalists in the industry, but perhaps in the 21st-century online media environment, they are the skills required to create "virtual news."

Project Veritas has also employed a former MI6 spy to train aspiring undercover "journalists" in surreptitious and evasive techniques. The spy has reportedly established a training camp and recently trained a couple to pose as new donors to the Wyoming Democrat Party. Investigations by *NPR* reporter Adam Goldman[16] revealed that the journalist recruitment and training took place on a ranch owned by former Blackwater CEO and conservative activist Erik Prince.[17,18,19]

To distinguish himself as a superior journalist, O'Keefe has also spent considerable time and resources conducting stings against mainstream news outlets, including *CNN*, the *New York Times*, and the *Washington Post*. For example, in 2017, again relying on deceptive methods to lure his target, he posed as a Muslim activist seeking to produce content that was strongly politically Islamic. He succeeded in eliciting an anti-Muslim reaction from an NPR fund-raising executive. The exposé caused two NPR executives to be fired and one resigned.[20,21]

Project Veritas is also openly challenging mainstream media's established rules of the road. For example, its website mentions the ethical guidelines of the Society of Professional Journalists (SPJ), the largest association for journalists in the United States, on undercover journalism. Those standards provide that journalists should "avoid undercover or other surreptitious methods of gathering information unless traditional, open methods will not yield information vital to the public."[22] *Project Veritas* has countered the SPJ position, arguing that undercover techniques are not only allowed but required.[23]

The SPJ ethical guidelines also advise journalists to "label advocacy and commentary."[24] O'Keefe's doctored scandals are clearly advocacy pieces, written, staged, and selectively edited as *exposés*. They are also produced using unconventional surprise techniques to catch their targets off guard and put them in the worst possible light. He nevertheless passes his work off as genuine journalism.

SPJ urges journalists to "provide context." But O'Keefe's videos deliberately decontextualized content. So, they are of limited credibility. His work, indeed, ironically belies the moniker *Veritas* (or truth, in Latin).

By revealing supposed sordid secrets and hypocrisy by staff at large social service agencies such as *Planned Parenthood* and *ACORN*, O'Keefe may be able to assert that he is addressing corruption, inefficiency, fraud, or waste.[25] There is a history for that form of reporting. For example, in the 1980s psychiatric institutions around the country were shut down in favor of community facilities after a series of scandals revealing the squalor of many psychiatric asylums.[26]

But O'Keefe's use of deception and strategic editing merely cause harm, stigmatizing and labeling those he captures on camera as untrustworthy or corrupt. His works do not address the systemic issues endemic to large government programs. Moreover, for those impugned by his videos, when "salvation" comes after months or years of investigations, if ever, their spoiled identities are already seared in the memory of the public.[27]

Whether a journalist or not, O'Keefe is manufacturing scandals that, upon investigation, have been found baseless. These "scandals" nonetheless endure on the internet as a proven fact in perpetuity, stigmatizing unwitting targets and creating indelible mistrust in the public eye.

O'Keefe's use of miniaturized digital cameras and platforms such as Breitbart.com—and until he was permanently banned—Twitter.com enable his "gotcha" videos to not only go viral but to persist on the internet's virtual information ecosystem. Thus, although there is perhaps nothing new about this type of character harassment, about unscrupulous individuals willing to manipulate reality to their own devices, when our modern communications technology is left in the hands of the likes of O'Keefe, it affords them a stunning degree of power to conduct political control through punishment and labeling.

Scholar Brian Michael Goss notes that *Project Veritas*' ability to smear political foes is much more pernicious than true scandals such as Watergate or the Lewinsky/Clinton Affair.[28] This is because *Project Veritas*' scandals are manufactured and designed to use the technologies of this information age to foment constant political harassment. Goss calls this malign activity "flak." He believes that—unlike real political scandals that compel the exposed individuals or organizations to repent and reform by reducing corruption and becoming more transparent and responsive—flak artists such as *Project Veritas* merely corrode trust in our political and government institutions, by polarizing audiences and undermining the effectiveness and morale of civic institutions and individuals. But they are disrupters of the established ways of "doing news" in the news world.

These digital developments have sweepingly altered the "understandings embodied in the common practices" of the news world.[29] Those common practices now under threat have been the bedrock of the Fourth Estate and the public has greatly come to rely on them to reach a core foundation of American democracy. But how are these new, deceptive practices coming to the fore? Their prominence corresponds to what Howard Becker wrote in 1982 about "art worlds." Becker argued that artists who are viewed as "singular" successes for their creativity and ingenuity in fact rely on an entire network and industry of menial and specialized workers who contribute to the artists' successes. Those support systems harmonize a set of conventions that not only bring art from idea to the market but also help decide what is and is not considered art.

For the virtual mass media, instead of art, the work at hand is the new, *virtual*, news. The veneer of the David versus Goliath narrative in O'Keefe's portrayal of himself as a small operation producing piercing solo videos to disable large corrupt political machines is little more than a fig leaf. Behind the most successful proliferation of virtual news outlets such as O'Keefe's is a chain of wealthy benefactors and influential alt-right political activists promoting and supporting their flak.

For example, Andrew Breitbart, founder of the alt-right online media platform *Breitbart News*, was firmly in O'Keefe's corner as far back as his first "gotcha" journalism production targeting Planned Parenthood in 2008. In a 2010 interview with *CBS News*, Breitbart, by then a well-known albeit controversial media figure, gave O'Keefe's *exposés* maximal exposure.

REDEFINING CONVENTION

What makes the likes of O'Keefe so notable is that they are shaking up the definition of the news itself and changing how society establishes the fact. Since the emergence of the internet and the miniaturization of video and audio equipment, unconventional "home-grown" outfits such as O'Keefe's have emerged, become powerful, and are increasingly dominating the news landscape.

O'Keefe's work has emerged at a time when the internet, mobile computing devices, and computerized data have revolutionized the speed with which news travels, the media upon which news is distributed, and the mechanisms for funding it. It is a sea change, and the 20th-century conventional mainstream media are now increasingly viewed as staid institutions hardly capable of keeping up with the new media environments that are the stomping grounds for the O'Keefes and Breitbarts of the world.

In response to those sweeping changes, mainstream news media executives are now debating the very essence of their work, especially what influence should narratives—particularly patently biased narratives and heavily curated and decontextualized videos—have over the way the industry assesses news?

In some respects, it appears the conventional media are groping for solutions and simply throwing ideas onto the screen. For example, one less-than-conventional feature of the emerging news landscape is the online publication by conventional news outlets of consumer comments using native and third-party applications on newspaper websites.[30,31] The mainstream news outlets have, indeed, capitalized on these comment sections—with their often controversial, over-the-top, adversarial and argumentative banter between commenters—because of the traffic they attract that also translates into advertising dollars. Are the conventional media merely conceding? Are they turning over the keys to the kingdom?

Recent studies have shown that the growing distrust of mainstream media and, hence government, especially by right-leaning media consumers is rooted not only in disputes over the facts reported by these long-standing institutions but also in the entire epistemological foundation upon which knowledge production and fact-checking is based.[32,33]

The new "virtual" news creators have turned the standards and methods by which facts are distinguished from fiction and/or opinion on their ears. Doctored videos and scandalous claims produced by heavily biased sources with scant factual context have become part of the public discourse. They have simultaneously diminished the credibility and meaning of news itself.

But O'Keefe's distortion of facts into doctored fiction is not unlike the throngs of adversarial commenters who dispute the credibility of every news article in long mainstream media online reader/commenter threads, and that adversarial commenting and rhetoric detracts from users' perceptions of the credibility of the reported news itself.[34,35]

Andrew Breitbart once admitted O'Keefe's clownishness by comparing him to Borat. But O'Keefe, Breitbart, and, now, their attorneys and funders are pushing the news industry to not only accept their tactics as journalism but to accept their narratives—regardless of whether they are at odds with the observed facts—as "news."

The debate within mainstream media over how much to adapt to the disruptive influences of virtual news producers is troubling. And it appears the standards of journalism are indeed changing. For example, in 2012, when right-wing news media veteran and mogul Rupert Murdoch played fast and loose with journalistic ethics, he became embroiled in a scandal of epic proportions.[36] After revelations that they hacked the voice mails and the emails of their targets, including politicians and, in one case, a young woman who was the victim of murder, his tabloid, *News of the World*, then the UK's most popular tabloid, was shut down.[37] Murdoch drew a sharp line around the illegality and immorality of these activities in open testimony to lawmakers. But undercover video (not by O'Keefe) caught him making impromptu remarks in which he stated that law enforcement was incompetent and targeted him unfairly.[38,39] No such impacts have yet befallen *Project Veritas* and Breitbart News. Quite to the contrary, their influence is rising.

THE FUTURE OF NEWS

As the 21st century enters its third decade, traditional and "new" news outlets all realize that, as clownish as O'Keefe seems, his approach is having profound implications on the future of journalism. Stings, after all, were not entirely unheard of in the early days of mass media, hence the SPJ standard, and they were used on broadcast TV news magazines for decades.[40]

Although conventional news outlets have been reluctant to resort to such tactics, they are struggling to stay relevant, including revisiting both facts and ethics, Moreover, as more virtual news creators come onto the stage, they will continue to rattle the establishment's cage with the new digital technologies. The conventional news business will, therefore, have to adapt or move on.

But the battle is still on, and O'Keefe has recently become the story. In November of 2021, O'Keefe's home and work sites were raided by the FBI, and his mobile devices were confiscated on charges of trafficking in stolen material. What is being reported as of this writing is that O'Keefe had allegedly been tipped off in 2020 about a diary and other material supposedly abandoned in a Florida apartment that had been vacated by Ashley Biden, the youngest adult child of President Joseph Biden and First Lady Jill Biden. After some due diligence, O'Keefe decided not to run the story. He also submitted the diary and other effects to local law enforcement officials. Over one year later, O'Keefe was raided by the FBI for trafficking in stolen material.[41]

O'Keefe's attorneys are portraying him as a *bona fide* investigative journalist deserving protection of news sources and donors lists. In a November 2021 memorandum to judge Annelise Torres of the US District Court for the Southern District of New York, the attorneys compared O'Keefe to journalists Nellie Bly, Mike Wallace, and Ken Silverstein. They argued that pressure to maximize profits has driven the conventional broadcast media to abandon investigative journalism, but that O'Keefe is filling the void using non-traditional, undercover tactics to obtain his stories.[42] The US government's position is that O'Keefe is not engaged in "journalism" within any traditional or accepted definition of the term.

That case and the fact that O'Keefe has spent much energy conducting stings and becoming embroiled in lawsuits, including against traditional media outlets such as the *New York Times* and the *Washington Post*, has brought the controversy about what constitutes journalism, into greater focus. For example, turning the tables on O'Keefe, shortly after the FBI raids of November 2021, the *New York Times* published an *exposé* about the raid against *Project Veritas.*[43] That led O'Keefe to sue the *New York Times* for defamation, asserting that the *Times* had relied on information leaked by the FBI about the raids.[44]

In an ironic twist to the story, O'Keefe's attorneys are now accusing the FBI of going around "established legal practice" to determine whether O'Keefe is a journalist, including using the internet to find bloggers and politically motivated competitors to build their case against.[45,46,47,48,49] In addition, although O'Keefe has never hesitated to leave exculpatory footage out of his accusatory videos, his attorneys are now accusing the prosecutors of doing the same.[50,51]

O'Keefe's attorneys are also challenging the FBI's overreach because the materials seized include materials that are unrelated to the diary story.[52,53,54] The attorneys claim that the prosecution obtained search warrants for accused material under legal reasons from which journalists are exempted, concluding that O'Keefe has always demonstrated fidelity to a set of "journalistic ethics" that include "high editorial standards."[55]

O'Keefe stands to benefit greatly from these recent events because, apparently, journalists, politicians, and the American Civil Liberties Union (ACLU) agree, at least in part, that the FBI case is raising legitimate questions about what constitutes journalism. The question of whether O'Keefe is a journalist in the eyes of the law is also central to *Project Veritas*' lawsuit against the *New York Times.*

Ranking member of the Senate Judiciary Committee Charles Grassley (R-IA) has gone on record concerned that the FBI's dawn raid included the extraction of protected information and characterized the FBI's actions as heavy handed. Grassley also questioned whether the FBI leaked information on the documents to the *New York Times.*[56] The ACLU has similarly chimed in stating that, although *Project Veritas*' methods are "disgraceful," the case is nevertheless consequential for press freedom.[57]

So, where does this all end? Objectivity in news reporting is clearly being challenged by the growing competition among so many politically tinged media outlets and amateur reporters for the public's eyes and ears. The boundaries of what constitutes journalism are shifting dramatically and quickly, with conservative organizational support for new media outlets and "gotcha" journalism out-competing those more conventional journalistic outlets still trying to stay within the ethical lanes.

But a scoop, is a scoop, is a scoop, and the more outlandish, the more controversial the reporting, the greater the audience. So, remaining in the business will require concessions. As evolving technology, micro-level access to the bully pulpit, extreme political agendas, and sensational content production continues to rile news worlds, objectivity and truth are being altered, and the networks and collectives of multifaceted newsmakers, editors, journalists, and publishers are haltingly adapting to the new paradigm in truth, fact, and news production.

NOTES

1. Drucker, David, "Palin Makes Her Case Before Adoring Crowd," *Roll Call,* September 3, 2008.

2. Kotz, David, "Great Recession of 2008 and After." In *The Oxford Encyclopedia of American Business, Labor, and Economic History* (Oxford University Press, 2013).

3. Trefis Team, "Market Crashes Compared: -28% Coronavirus Crash Vs. 4 Historic Market Crashes," *Forbes,* March 13, 2020.

4. Hogberg, David, "NACA: Neighborhood Assistance Corporation of America ACORN's Rival in Shakedown Tactics," *Capital Research,* September 2009.

5. ACORN, "ACORN: 1970-1975," *Way Back When Machine,* 2008.

6. Rivas, Dan, "ACORN Closing Its Doors," *The Non Profit Times,* March 23, 2010.

7. Alinsky, Saul David, *Rules for Radicals: A Practical Primer for Realistic Radicals* (New York: Vintage Books, 1972), 130.

8. Olshan, Jeremy, "'Pimp & Hooker' Catch B'klyn Staff," *New York Post,* September 14, 2009.

9. Friedersdorf, Conor, "Andrew Breitbart and James O'Keefe Ruined Him, and Now He Gets $100,000," *The Atlantic,* November 22, 2019.

10. Friedersdorf, "Andrew Breitbart and James O'Keefe Ruined Him, and Now He Gets $100,000."

11. Olshan, "'Pimp & Hooker' Catch B'klyn Staff."

12. Staff, Fox News, "Third Videotape Reveals ACORN Assisting 'Pimp,' 'Prostitute' in Brooklyn, N.Y.," *Fox News,* March 25, 2015.

13. Olshan, "'Pimp & Hooker' Catch B'klyn Staff."

14. Olshan, "'Pimp & Hooker' Catch B'klyn Staff."

15. Staff, Project Veritas. "Overview," *ProjectVeritas.Com,* 2010.

16. Davies, Dave. "How a Former Spy Trained Conservatives to Infiltrate Progressive Groups," *NPR News,* July 2, 2021.

17. Davies, "How a Former Spy Trained Conservatives to Infiltrate Progressive Groups."

18. Goldman, Adam, and Mark Mazzetti, "Project Veritas and the Line Between Journalism and Political Spying," *The New York Times,* November 11, 2021.

19. Schmidt, Michael S., William K. Rashbaum, Precioujs Fondren, and Adam Goldman, "People Tied to Project Veritas Scrutinized in Theft of Diary From Biden's Daughter," *The New York Times,* November 5, 2021.

20. Farhi, Paul, "Secretly Recorded Phone Calls Cast NPR Fundraiser in Unflattering Light," *The Washington Post,* March 10, 2011.

21. Staff, Fox News, "Third Videotape Reveals ACORN Assisting 'Pimp,' 'Prostitute' in Brooklyn, N.Y."

22. Society of Professional Journalists Staff, "SPJ Code of Ethics - Society of Professional Journalists," *Society of Professional Journalists,* 2021. Accessed December 30, 2021. https://www.spj.org/ethicscode.asp.

23. Staff, Project Veritas, "Overview."

24. SPJ Staff, "SPJ Code of Ethics - Society of Professional Journalists," 2021.

25. Theimer, Sharon, and Peter Yost, "Did ACORN Get Too Big for Its Own Good?" *NBC News,* 2009. Accessed September 19, 2019.

26. Leff, Julian, "Deinstitutionalization, Psychiatry of." In *International Encyclopedia of the Social & Behavioral Sciences* (2nd edition), edited by James D. Wright, 47–51 (Oxford: Elsevier, 2015).

27. Goffman, Erving, *Stigma: Notes on the Management of Spoiled Identity* (New York: Simon & Schuster, 1963/2009).

28. Goss, Brian Michael, "Veritable Flak Mill: A case study of Project Veritas and a call for Truth," *Journalism studies (London, England)* 19 (2008): 548–563.

29. Becker, H. S., *Art Worlds* (Los Angeles: University of California Press, 1982).

30. Conlin, Lindsey, and Chris Roberts, "Presence of Online Reader Comments Lowers News Site Credibility," *Newspaper Research Journal* 37 (2016): 365–376.

31. Waddell, T. Franklin, "What Does the Crowd Think? How Online Comments and Popularity Metrics Affect News Credibility and Issue Importance," *New Media & Society* 20 (2018): 3068–3083.

32. Benkler, Yochai, Robert Farris, and Hal Roberts, *Network Propaganda* (New York: Oxford University Press, 2018).

33. Tripodi, Francesca Bolla, "ReOpen Demands as Public Health Threat: A Sociotechnical Framework for Understanding the Stickiness of Misinformation," *Computational and Mathematical Organization Theory* (2021).

34. Conlin and Roberts, "Presence of Online Reader Comments Lowers News Site Credibility."

35. Waddell, "What Does the Crowd Think?"

36. Abbas, Mohammed, and Kate Holton, "British Police Arrest Five at Murdoch's Sun Newspaper," *Reuters,* February 11, 2012.

37. Abbas and Holton, "British Police Arrest Five at Murdoch's Sun Newspaper."

38. Staff, NPR, "Murdoch Says He Was Misled About Tabloid Scandal," *NPR News*, July 19, 2011.

39. Whalen, Jeanne, "Rupert Murdoch Remarks Secretly Recorded," *Wall Street Journal,* July 4, 2013.

40. Gerstein, Josh, "FBI Raid on Project Veritas Founder's Home Sparks Questions about Press Freedom," *POLITICO* (November 11, 2013).

41. Gerstein, "FBI Raid on Project Veritas Founder's Home Sparks Questions about Press Freedom."

42. Staff, Washington Post, "Project Veritas Response to DOJ," *Washington Post* (November 22, 2021).

43. Schmidt, Rashbaum, Fondren, and Goldman, "People Tied to Project Veritas Scrutinized in Theft of Diary from Biden's Daughter."

44. Staff, Washington Post, "Project Veritas Response to DOJ."

45. Flood, Brian, "Project Veritas Legal Team Rips DOJ Raid of O'Keefe as 'Sucker Punch' to Free Press, Praises Unlikely Allies," *Fox News,* November 19, 2021.

46. Gerstein, "FBI Raid on Project Veritas Founder's Home Sparks Questions about Press Freedom."

47. Schmidt, Rashbaum, Fondren, and Goldman, "People Tied to Project Veritas Scrutinized in Theft of Diary From Biden's Daughter."

48. Staff, Washington Post, "Project Veritas Response to DOJ."

49. Ward, Myah, "Appeals Court Rules New York Times Can Temporarily Keep Project Veritas Documents," *POLITICO,* December 28, 2021.

50. Gerstein, "FBI Raid on Project Veritas Founder's Home Sparks Questions about Press Freedom."

51. Ward, "Appeals Court Rules New York Times Can Temporarily Keep Project Veritas Documents."

52. Grassley, Charles, "Sen. Grassley Demands Answers in DOJ's and FBI's Heavy-Handed Targeting of Project Veritas," *United States Senate Judiciary Committee,* November 17, 2021.

53. Flood, "Project Veritas Legal Team Rips DOJ Raid of O'Keefe as 'Sucker Punch' to Free Press, Praises Unlikely Allies."

54. Staff, Washington Post, "Project Veritas Response to DOJ."

55. Staff, Washington Post, "Project Veritas Response to DOJ."

56. Grassley, "Sen. Grassley Demands Answers in DOJ's and FBI's Heavy-Handed Targeting of Project Veritas."

57. Hauss, Brian, "ACLU Comment on FBI Raid of Project Veritas Founder," *American Civil Liberties Union,* November 14, 2021.

Conclusion

Bringing together the various theories and strands of this volume, it is clear that one main reason consumers use social media to target others for punishment is that they accidentally encounter conflict while expressing their own worldviews online. Self-expression, especially of deeply held values, stems from the human quest for acknowledgment. This quest also occurs in the physical world. But the current generation of text- and visual-media-based social platforms such as Facebook and Twitter promote online conflict due to the limited and one-dimensional ways their software aggregate users and distribute feeds among friends and strangers alike. On these platforms, people who do not know one another gather around single issues or interests and get into written "conversation" about deeply held views. This spells a recipe for interpersonal misunderstanding and conflict. Few opportunities exist within the same groups to learn about other cross-cutting commonalities unless users choose to engage one another offline.

In addition, the swiftness with which information travels means that calls to target others occur very quickly. Moreover, everyone claiming to be a journalist, and some legitimate news sources, use photos and videos to provide proof of facts that are not properly contextualized, further fanning the flames of misunderstanding and conflict.

Over the last 40 years, electronic media have gradually displaced our sense of space and place by dispersing the public and private, and the "backstage" from the "front stage." Online users not only sometimes lose control of who gets to see private information about them, but social media enables deceptively-minded users to also create completely false personae that could be used to punish or extort others.

Perhaps these are reasons why social media platforms such as Twitter and Facebook (Meta) have already invested heavily in virtual reality platforms, possibly giving the opportunity to use the meta provide greater context across user communities than currently possible. For the time being, media literacy about the shortcomings of social media and knowledge of the quest for acknowledgment as a trigger for pursuing online conflict combined with greater transparency about privacy controls of user profiles can go a long way to deescalate online conflict.

Bibliography

AARP. "Fake Dating Profiles Used to Lure Women in Dating Scam." AARP. https://www.aarp.org/podcasts/the-perfect-scam/info-2019/online-dating-scam.html.

Abbas, Mohammed, and Kate Holton. 2012. "British Police Arrest Five at Murdoch's Sun Newspaper." *Reuters*. 11 February 2012, sec. Media Industry News. https://www.reuters.com/article/us-britain-newscorp-arrests-idUSTRE81A07T20120211.

"ACORN: 1970–1975." 2008. Archived Website. Association of Community Organizations for Reform Now. 14 October 2008. https://web.archive.org/web/20081014021233/http://www.acorn.org/index.php?id=12447.

ADL Staff. "Two Years Ago, They Marched in Charlottesville. Where Are They Now?" 8-8-2019. Anti-Defamation League. Accessed 9 June 2022. https://www.adl.org/resources/blog/two-years-ago-they-marched-charlottesville-where-are-they-now.

Alinsky, Saul David. *Rules for Radicals: A Practical Primer for Realistic Radicals*. New York: Vintage Books, 1972.

Andeweg, Rudy B. "Consociationalism." In *International Encyclopedia of the Social & Behavioral Sciences* (2nd edition), edited by James D. Wright, 692–94. Oxford: Elsevier, 2015.

Anti-Defamation League Staff. "14 Words." ADL.ORG. 3 May 2022. https://www.adl.org/resources/hate-symbol/14-words.

Associated Press. "Covington Catholic HS Students Were Not Instigators in Confrontational Video, Kentucky Bishop Says." ABC11 Raleigh-Durham. 20 February 2019. https://abc11.com/5136720/.

Beam, Adam, and Brian Melley. "Teens in 'MAGA' Hats Mock Native American." *Daily Hampshire Gazette*. 20 January 2019. https://www.gazettenet.com/Students-in-MAGA-hats-mock-Native-American-after-rally-22906554.

Becker, Ernest. *The Birth and Death of Meaning: A Perspective in Psychiatry and Anthropology*. New York: Free Press of Glencoe, 1962.

Becker, H.S. *Art Worlds*. Los Angeles: University of California Press, 1982.

Beckett, Lois. "How Richard Spencer's Home Town Weathered a Neo-Nazi 'Troll Storm.'" *The Guardian*. 5 February 2017, sec. US news. https://www.theguardian.com/us-news/2017/feb/05/richard-spencer-whitefish-neo-nazi-march.

Bekiempis, Victoria. "Covington Catholic High Apologizes for Students Who Mocked Native American Veteran During March for Life." *The Daily Beast*. 19 January 2019, sec. us-news. https://www.thedailybeast.com/the-native-american-mocked-by-kentucky-high-school-students-in-dc-is-military-veteran-nathan-phillips.

Benkler, Yochai, Robert Farris, and Hal Roberts. *Network Propaganda*. New York: Oxford University Press, 2018.

Bergman, Shawn M., Matthew E. Fearrington, Shaun W. Davenport, and Jacqueline Z. Bergman. "Millennials, Narcissism, and Social Networking: What Narcissists Do on Social Networking Sites and Why." *Personality and Individual Differences* 50, no. 5 (2010): 706–11. doi: 10.1016/j.paid.2010.12.022.

Blanch, Joey L., and Wesley L. Hsu. "An Introduction to Violent Crime on the Internet." In *United States Attorneys' Bulletin* 64 (2016): 2.

Bogost, Ian. "Stop Trusting Viral Videos." *The Atlantic*. 21 January 2019. https://www.theatlantic.com/technology/archive/2019/01/viral-clash-students-and-native-americans-explained/580906/.

boyd, danah. "Truth, Lies, and 'Doxxing': The Real Moral of the Gawker/Reddit Story." *Wired*. 29 October 2012. https://www.wired.com/2012/10/truth-lies-doxxing-internet-vigilanteism/.

Brookbank, Sarah. "Analysis: What the Video from the Incident at the Indigenous Peoples March Tell Us about What Happened." News. *The Enquirer*. 20 January 2019. https://www.cincinnati.com/story/news/2019/01/20/analyzing-video-incident-indigenous-peoples-march/2631412002/.

Brown, Dalvin. "Twitter's Cancel Culture: A Force for Good or a Digital Witchhunt? The Answer Is Complicated." *USA Today*. 17 July 2020. https://www.usatoday.com/story/tech/2020/07/17/has-twitters-cancel-culture-gone-too-far/5445804002/.

Bullingham, Liam, and Ana C. Vasconcelos. "'The Presentation of Self in the Online World': Goffman and the Study of Online Identities." *Journal of Information Science* 39, no. 1 (2013): 101–12. doi: 10.1177/0165551512470051.

Carpenter, Christopher J. "Narcissism on Facebook: Self-Promotional and Anti-Social Behavior." *Personality and Individual Differences* 52, no. 4 (2012): 482–86. doi: 10.1016/j.paid.2011.11.011.

Castillo, Bernal Diaz Del. *The Conquest of New Spain*. Translated by John M. Cohen. London: Penguin Books, 1521/1963.

Chapell, Bill. "Differing Narratives After Standoff Between Native American Man, High School Student." NPR.ORG. 21 January 2019. https://www.npr.org/2019/01/21/687134573/differing-narratives-after-standoff-between-native-american-man-high-school-stud.

CNN, Sara Sidner. "Native American Elder Nathan Phillips, in His Own Words." CNN. 21 January 2019. https://www.cnn.com/2019/01/21/us/nathan-phillips-maga-teens-interview/index.html.

Conlin, Lindsey, and Chris Roberts. "Presence of Online Reader Comments Lowers News Site Credibility." *Newspaper Research Journal* 37, no. 4 (2016): 365–76. doi: 10.1177/0739532916677056.

Cowicide, dir. 2019. "Guy with a MAGA Hat Mocking an Elder Native American Protestor at Indigenous Peoples March." *Youtube.Com*. https://www.youtube.com/watch?v=5FogNIr2x40.

Dan Hassert. "Mayor Meyer: Covington 'Appalled.'" City of Covington, KY. 19 January 2019. https://www.covingtonky.gov/news/2019/01/19/mayor-meyer-covington-appalled.

Daniels, Elizabeth A. "Sexiness on Social Media: The Social Costs of Using a Sexy Profile Photo." *Sexualization, Media, & Society* 2, no. 4 (2016): 237. doi: 10.1177/2374623816683522.

Davies, Dave. "Anti-Semitism and the Soviet and Anti-Zionist Campaign." *Australian Left Review* 1, no. 76 (1981): 24–30.

Daw, Stephen. "A Complete Timeline of Kevin Hart's Oscar-Hosting Controversy, From Tweets to Apologies." *Billboard* (blog). 13 January 2020. https://www.billboard.com/music/awards/kevin-hart-oscar-hosting-controversy-timeline-8492982/.

Defender, DMCA. "South Korea Draws up Cyberbulling Laws after Second K-Pop Suicide." *DMCA Defender*. 30 December 2019. http://dmcadefender.com/south-korea-draws-up-cyberbulling-laws-after-second-k-pop-suicide/.

Drucker, David. "Palin Makes Her Case Before Adoring Crowd." *Roll Call*. 3 September 2008. https://www.rollcall.com/2008/09/03/palin-makes-her-case-before-adoring-crowd/.

Dubois, Ross. "The Strange and Sordid End of an A&M Professor." *Texas Monthly*. 27 March 2013. https://www.texasmonthly.com/articles/the-strange-and-sordid-end-of-an-am-professor/.

Dugas, Michelle, and Arie W. Kruglanski. "The Quest for Significance Model of Radicalization: Implications for the Management of Terrorist Detainees." *Behavioral Sciences & the Law* 32, no. 3 (2014): 423–39. doi: 10.1002/bsl.2122.

Durkheim, É. *The Division of Labor in Society*. New York: Free Press Paperback, 1964.

Ellefson, Lindsey. "Alexi McCammond Returns to MSNBC After Teen Vogue Exit (Video)." 13 May 2021. https://www.thewrap.com/alexi-mccammond-msnbc-appearance/.

Farhi, Paul. "Secretly Recorded Phone Calls Cast NPR Fundraiser in Unflattering Light," 11 March 2011. http://www.washingtonpost.com/wp-dyn/content/article/2011/03/10/AR2011031005119.html.

———. "The Washington Post Sued by Family of Covington Catholic Teenager." *Washington Post*. 19 February 2019. https://www.washingtonpost.com/lifestyle/style/the-washington-post-sued-by-family-of-covington-catholic-teenager/2019/02/19/aa252be4-349c-11e9-854a-7a14d7fec96a_story.html.

Feiner, Lauren. "Facebook Explains Why Its A.I. Didn't Detect the New Zealand Mosque Shooting Video before It Was Viewed 4,000 Times." *CNBC*. 21 March 2019. https://www.cnbc.com/2019/03/21/why-facebooks-ai-didnt-detect-the-new-zealand-mosque-shooting-video.html.

Fisher, Jim. “Jim Fisher True Crime: Professor James Aune Chose Death Over Disgrace.” *Jim Fisher True Crime* (blog). 28 August 2020. https://jimfisher-truecrime.blogspot.com/2013/03/professor-james-aune-chose-death-over.html.

Flanagan, Caitlin. “The Media Botched the Covington Catholic Story.” *The Atlantic*. 23 January 2019. https://www.theatlantic.com/ideas/archive/2019/01/media-must-learn-covington-catholic-story/581035/.

Flood, Allison. “Young Adult Author Cancels Own Novel after Race Controversy.” News. *The Guardian*. 1 February 2019. http://www.theguardian.com/books/2019/feb/01/young-adult-author-cancels-own-novel-after-race-controversy.

Foucault, Michel. *Discipline and Punish: The Birth of the Prison*. New York: Vintage Books, a division of Random House, 1979.

Fox, Jesse, and Margaret C. Rooney. “The Dark Triad and Trait Self-Objectification as Predictors of Men’s Use and Self-Presentation Behaviors on Social Networking Sites.” *Personality and Individual Differences* 76 (April 2015): 161–65. doi: 10.1016/j.paid.2014.12.017.

Fox News Staff. “Third Videotape Reveals ACORN Assisting ‘Pimp,’ ‘Prostitute’ in Brooklyn, N.Y..” News. *Fox News*. 14 September 2009. https://www.foxnews.com/story/third-videotape-reveals-acorn-assisting-pimp-prostitute-in-brooklyn-n-y.

French, Laura. “The Social Media Age: More Suicides, Violent Acts Streamed Live.” *Forensic Magazine*, February 2017.

Friedersdorf, Conor. “Andrew Breitbart and James O’Keefe Ruined Him, and Now He Gets $100,000.” *The Atlantic*. 8 March 2013. https://www.theatlantic.com/politics/archive/2013/03/andrew-breitbart-and-james-okeefe-ruined-him-and-now-he-gets-100-000/273841/.

Gerstein, Josh. “FBI Raid on Project Veritas Founder’s Home Sparks Questions about Press Freedom - POLITICO.” *Politico*. 13 November 2021. https://www.politico.com/news/2021/11/13/raid-veritas-okeefe-biden-press-521307.

Goffman, Erving. *The Presentation of Self in Everyday Life*. New York: Anchor Books/Doubleday, 1999.

Goffman, Erving. *Stigma: Notes on the Management of Spoiled Identity*. New York: Simon and Schuster, 2009.

Goldman, Adam, and Mark Mazzetti. “Project Veritas and the Line Between Journalism and Political Spying.” *The New York Times*. 11 November 2021, sec. U.S. https://www.nytimes.com/2021/11/11/us/politics/project-veritas-journalism-political-spying.html.

Goldstein, Barry M. “All Photos Lie: Images as Data.” In *Visual Research Methods: Image, Society, and Representation*, edited by Gregory C. Stanczak. Thousand Oaks: SAGE Publications, 2007.

Grasha, Kevin. “‘This Is a Dumb Tweet’: Nick Sandmann Fires Attorney Lin Wood after Twitter, Telegram Posts.” News Website. *Cincinnati Enquirer*. 26 January 2021. https://www.cincinnati.com/story/news/2021/01/26/nick-sandmann-fired-attorney-lin-wood-after-twitter-telegram-posts/4260538001/.

Grassley, Charles. “Sen. Grassley Demands Answers in DOJ’s and FBI’s Heavy-Handed Targeting of Project Veritas.” United States Senate Committee on the Judiciary. 17 November 2021. https://www.judiciary.senate.gov/press/rep/releases

/grassley-demands-answers-in-dojs-and-fbis-heavy-handed-targeting-of-project-veritas-personnel.

Gray Media Group. "CNN Settles Lawsuit with Covington Catholic Student Involved in Protest." https://www.kktv.com. 7 January 2020. https://www.kktv.com/content/news/CNN-settles-lawsuit-with-Covington-Catholic-student-involved-in-protest-566783941.html.

Greene, David. "Outcry Results After Video Appears to Show Students Mocking Native American Man." *NPR.ORG.* Morning Edition. 21 January 2019. https://www.npr.org/2019/01/21/687085976/outcry-results-after-video-appears-to-shows-students-mocking-native-american-man.

Hafezi, Parisa. "Iranian Media Outlets Add to Bounty for Killing Britain's Rushdie | Reuters." 22 February 2016. https://www.reuters.com/article/us-iran-rushdie/iranian-media-outlets-add-to-bounty-for-killing-britains-rushdie-idUSKCN0VV1TI.

Hankes, Keegan. "Eye of the Stormer." SPLC Intelligence Report. 9 February 2017. https://www.splcenter.org/fighting-hate/intelligence-report/2017/eye-stormer.

Haring, Bruce. "Alexi McCammond Returns To Axios As Political Reporter – Deadline." *Deadline.Com.* 3 July 2021. https://deadline.com/2021/07/alexi-mccammond-teen-vogue-returns-axios-political-reporter-1234785981/.

Hauss, Brian. "ACLU Comment on FBI Raid of Project Veritas Founder." *American Civil Liberties Union.* 14 November 2021. https://www.aclu.org/press-releases/aclu-comment-fbi-raid-project-veritas-founder.

Hern, Alex. "Facebook Live Is Changing the World - But Not in the Way It Hoped." *The Guardian.* 5 January 2017, sec. Technology. https://www.theguardian.com/technology/2017/jan/05/facebook-live-social-media-live-streaming.

Hogan, Bernie. "The Presentation of Self in the Age of Social Media: Distinguishing Performances and Exhibitions Online." *Bulletin of Science, Technology & Society* 30, no. 6 (2010): 377–86. doi: 10.1177/0270467610385893.

Hogberg, David. "NACA: Neighborhood Assistance Corporation of America ACORN's Rival in Shakedown Tactics." Capital Research Center. 16 September 2009. https://capitalresearch.org/article/naca-neighborhood-assistance-corporation-of-america-acorns-rival-in-shakedown-tactics/.

Hollenbaugh, Erin E. "Self-Presentation in Social Media: Review and Research Opportunities." *Review of Communication Research* 9 (2021): 80–98.

Howard, Brooke L. "NYPD Seeks Tips After Vicious Subway Attack Caught on Video." 22 March 2019. https://www.thedailybeast.com/nypd-seeks-tips-after-vicious-subway-attack-caught-on-video?ref=home.

Hoyle, Niharika Mandhana and Rhiannon. "Facebook Left Up Video of New Zealand Shootings for an Hour." *WSJ.* 21 March 2019. https://www.wsj.com/articles/facebook-our-ai-tools-failed-to-catch-new-zealand-attack-video-11553156141.

Investigation Discovery (ID) Channel. "Web of Lies - Online Education (The Story of Jim Aune)." Film. Investigation Discovery (ID) Channel. 8 August 2017. https://www.investigationdiscovery.com/tv-shows/web-of-lies/full-episodes/online-education, https://www.investigationdiscovery.com/tv-shows/web-of-lies/full-episodes/online-education.

ISIS, dir. 2015. *Warning, Extremely Graphic Video: ISIS Burns Hostage Alive*. http://video.foxnews.com/v/4030583977001/.

Jeremy Bentham. 1791. Panopticon; or, The Inspection House: Containing the Idea of a New Principle. Re-printed and sold by T. Payne. Accessed 21 July 2022. http://archive.org/details/panopticonorins00bentgoog.

Kan, Michael, "Why Facebook's AI Failed to Detect Video of New Zealand Shooting." *PCMAG*. 21 March 2019. https://www.pcmag.com/news/367318/why-facebooks-ai-failed-to-detect-video-of-new-zealand-shoo.

Kessler, Glenn. "The 'Very Fine People' at Charlottesville: Who Were They? - The Washington Post." *Washington Post*. 8 May 2020. https://www.washingtonpost.com/politics/2020/05/08/very-fine-people-charlottesville-who-were-they-2/.

Khoshsabk, Nastaran, and Jane Southcott. "Gender Identity and Facebook: Social Conservatism and Saving Face." *The Qualitative Report*; Fort Lauderdale 24, no. 4 (2019): 632–47.

Klinenberg, Eric. "Social Media Can't Replace Social Infrastructure." *The Nation*. 2 May 2019. https://www.thenation.com/article/archive/social-media-cant-replace-social-infrastructure/.

KnowYourMeme.Com Staff. "Dog Poo Girl." *Know Your Meme*. 2005. https://knowyourmeme.com/memes/dog-poo-girl.

Kotz, David M. "Great Recession of 2008 and After." In *The Oxford Encyclopedia of American Business, Labor, and Economic History*. Oxford University Press, 2013.

Králová, Jana. "What Is Social Death?" *Contemporary Social Science* 10, no. 3 (2015): 235–48. doi: 10.1080/21582041.2015.1114407.

Kruglanski, Arie W., Jocelyn J. Bélanger, Michele Gelfand, Rohan Gunaratna, Malkanthi Hettiarachchi, Fernando Reinares, Edward Orehek, Jo Sasota, and Keren Sharvit. "Terrorism—A (Self) Love Story: Redirecting the Significance Quest Can End Violence." *American Psychologist* 68, no. 7 (2013): 559–75. doi: 10.1037/a0032615.

Kruglanski, Arie W., Jocelyn J. Bélanger, and Rohan Gunaratna. "Significance Quest Theory of Radicalization." In *The Three Pillars of Radicalization*. New York: Oxford University Press, 2019.

———. *The Three Pillars of Radicalization: Needs, Narratives, and Networks*. Oxford University Press, 2019.

Lane, Jeffery. *The Digital Street*. New York: Oxford University Press, 2018.

Lee-Won, Roselyn J., Minsun Shim, Yeon Kyoung Joo, and Sung Gwan Park. "Who Puts the Best'Face' Forward on Facebook?: Positive Self-Presentation in Online Social Networking and the Role of Self-Consciousness, Actual-to-Total Friends Ratio, and Culture." *Computers in Human Behavior* 39 (October 2014): 413–23. doi: 10.1016/j.chb.2014.08.007.

Leff, Julian. "Deinstitutionalization, Psychiatry of." In *International Encyclopedia of the Social & Behavioral Sciences* (2nd edition), edited by James D. Wright, 47–51. London, Oxford: Elsevier, 2015.

Lenz, Ryan. "A Gathering of Eagles: Extremists Look to Montana." SPLC Intelligence Report. 15 November 2011. https://www.splcenter.org/fighting-hate/intelligence-report/2011/gathering-eagles-extremists-look-montana.

Leslie, Esther. "Walter Benjamin and the Birth of Photography." In *On Photography*. London: Reaktion Books, 2015.

Lewis, Helen. "Against the Rage Machine." *New Statesman*. 13 March 2015. 1664930216. ProQuest Central; Research Library. http://mutex.gmu.edu/login?url=https://www.proquest.com/magazines/against-rage-machine/docview/1664930216/se-2?accountid=14541.

Lijphart, Arend. *Democracy in Plural Societies: A Comparative Exploration*. Yale University Press, 2017.

Lin, Kimberly. "Salman Rushdie and the Iranian Fatwa." History. *Historic Mysteries* (blog). 16 September 2018. https://www.historicmysteries.com/salman-rushdie-fatwa/.

London, Matt. "'Covington Kid' Nick Sandmann Says He's Lived under 'Constant Threat' for over a Year." Text. Article. *Fox News*. 13 April 2020. https://www.foxnews.com/media/nick-sandmann-covington-lincoln-memorial-media.

Lozano, Juan. "Dad Denies Using Daughter in Child-Porn Extortion Plot after Professor's Suicide." *NBC News*, March 27, 2013. Accessed 21 July 2022. https://www.nbcnews.com/news/us-news/dad-denies-using-daughter-child-porn-extortion-plot-after-professors-flna1c9096660.

Lyu, Seong Ok. "Travel Selfies on Social Media as Objectified Self-Presentation." *Tourism Management* 54 (June 2016): 185–95. doi: 10.1016/j.tourman.2015.11.001.

MacFarquhar, Neil. "Jury Finds Rally Organizers Responsible for Charlottesville Violence." *The New York Times*. 23 November 2021, sec. U.S. https://www.nytimes.com/2021/11/23/us/charlottesville-rally-verdict.html.

Macklin, Graham. "The Christchurch Attacks: Livestream Terror in the Viral Video Age." Combating Terrorism Center at West Point. 18 July 2019. https://ctc.usma.edu/christchurch-attacks-livestream-terror-viral-video-age/.

McLuhan, M., Q. Fiore, and J. Agel. *The Medium Is the Massage: An Inventory of Effects*. San Francisco: HardWired, 1966/1996.

Merunkova, Lucie, and Josef Slerka. "Goffman's Theory as a Framework for Analysis of Self Presentation on Online Social Networks." *Masaryk University Journal of Law and Technology* 13, no. 2 (2019): 243–76.

Meyrowitz, J. *No Sense of Place: The Impact of Electronic Media on Social Behavior*. Oxford University Press, 1986.

Mullin, Joe. "Lawsuit: Neo-Nazi Website Owner Is Liable for Harassing Montana Real Estate Agent." *Ars Technica*. 20 April 2017. https://arstechnica.com/tech-policy/2017/04/neo-nazi-website-that-launched-a-troll-storm-is-sued-for-harassment/.

Nashrullah, Tasneem. "Neo-Nazis Target Jewish Families In White Nationalist Leader's Hometown." *BuzzFeed News*. 18 December 2016. https://www.buzzfeednews.com/article/tasneemnashrulla/neo-nazis-target-jewish-families-and-establishments-in-monta.

New England Historical Society. "Way More Than the Scarlet Letter: Puritan Punishments." *New England Historical Society* (blog). 21 September 2015. http://www.newenglandhistoricalsociety.com/way-more-than-the-scarlet-letter-puritan-punishments/.

NPR Staff. "Murdoch Says He Was Misled About Tabloid Scandal: NPR." National Public Radio. 18 July 2011. https://www.npr.org/2011/07/19/138501685/u-k-to-question-key-figures-in-tabloid-scandal.

Olshan, Jeremy. "'Pimp & Hooker' Catch B'klyn Staff." *New York Post*. 14 September 2009. https://nypost.com/2009/09/14/pimp-hooker-catch-bklyn-staff/.

Osborn, Alex Faickney. *Your Creative Power: How to Use Imagination*. C. Scribner"s Sons, 1948.

Padilla, Mariel. "Daily Stormer Founder Should Pay 'Troll Storm' Victim $14 Million, Judge Says." *New York Times*. 16 July 2019. https://www.nytimes.com/2019/07/16/us/daily-stormer-lawsuit.html.

Pasquini, Maria. "Native American Veteran Says He Tried to Keep Peace as MAGA-Hat-Wearing Teens Harassed Him." *PEOPLE.Com*. 19 January 2019. https://people.com/politics/maga-hat-wearing-teenagers-harass-native-american-veteran/.

Patterson, Orlando. *Slavery and Social Death: A Comparative Study*. Fulcrum.Org. Boston: Harvard University Press, 1982.

PEN America. "PEN Outraged by Confinement of South African Writer Who Expressed Admiration for Rushdie." *PEN America* (blog). 11 April 2015. https://pen.org/pen-outraged-by-confinement-of-south-african-writer-who-expressed-admiration-for-rushdie/.

Phillips, Whitney. "The Oxygen of Amplification." *Digital Sociology*. Data & Society. Data & Society Research Institute. 22 May 2018. https://datasociety.net/library/oxygen-of-amplification/.

Project Veritas Staff. "Overview." *Project Veritas*. 2010. https://www.projectveritas.com/about/.

Quinn, Liam. "Nick Sandmann's Attorney Reveals Lawsuit against CNN." *NewsComAu*. 10 March 2019. https://www.news.com.au/finance/business/media/cnn-to-be-sued-for-more-than-355m-over-vicious-and-direct-attacks-on-covington-high-student-lawyer/news-story/c0807eb51d4aa06a5a4c0688a6c474fc#.opd8f.

Raftery, Brian. "Kevin Hart's Tweets Didn't Doom Him—His Messy Apology Did." *Wired*. 7 December 2018. https://www.wired.com/story/kevin-hart-oscars-tweets/.

REACTION FR, dir. 2019. *FULL 1h30 Video: Covington Catholic Students MAGA Hat Kids vs Nathan Phillips*. https://www.youtube.com/watch?v=3-pFMZaw5f0.

Rheingold, Howard. *Smart Mobs: The Next Social Revolution*. Cambridge, MA: Perseus Pub, 2002.

Richardson, Valerie. "Ex-CNN Host 'Likely' to Be Sued over Now-Deleted 'Punchable Face' Tweet: Sandmann Attorney." *The Washington Times*. 13 January 2020. https://www.washingtontimes.com/news/2020/jan/13/reza-aslan-likely-be-sued-over-now-deleted-punchab/.

Rivas, Dan. "ACORN Closing Its Doors - The NonProfit Times." 23 March 2010. https://www.thenonprofittimes.com/npt_articles/acorn-closing-its-doors/.

Robertson, Katie. "Teen Vogue Staff Members Condemn Editor's Decade-Old, Racist Tweets." *The New York Times*. 9 March 2021, sec. Business. https://www.nytimes.com/2021/03/09/business/media/teen-vogue-alexi-mccammond-tweets.html.

Rogan, Randall G. "Acknowledgment as a Primary Motive for Violent Extremism." Wake Forest, NC, 2018.

Rogan, Randall G. “Quest for Immortality: An Analysis of ISIS’s Dabiq.” *International Journal of Communication* 13 (2019): 20.

Romero, Dennis. “Covington Bishop Apologizes to Teen in Face-off with Native American.” *NBC News*. 25 January 2019. https://www.nbcnews.com/news/us-news/bishop-apologizes-teen-who-faced-native-american-n963056.

Ronson, Jon. *So You’ve Been Publicly Shamed*. New York: Penguin Publishing Group, 2016.

Ross, Drew A.R. “Backstage with the Knowledge Boys and Girls: Goffman and Distributed Agency in an Organic Online Community.” *Organization Studies* 28, no. 3 (2007): 307–25. doi: 10.1177/0170840607076000.

Rushdie, Salman. *Joseph Anton: A Memoir* (1st edition). New York: Random House, 2012.

Samuels, Alexandra. “Some People Want to Cancel Skai Jackson After She ‘Doxed’ a 13-Year-Old.” *The Daily Dot*. 11 August 2020. https://www.dailydot.com/irl/skai-jackson-dox/.

Sankin, Aaron. “Where in the World Is America’s Leading Neo-Nazi Troll?” *Reveal*. 27 July 2017. http://revealnews.org/blog/where-in-the-world-is-americas-leading-neo-nazi-troll/.

Schauer, Frederick F. *Profiles, Probabilities, and Stereotypes*. Boston: Harvard University Press, 2009.

Schiller, Dane. “Man Sentenced for Luring Professor into Online Relationship.” *HoustonChronicle.Com*. 19 November 2013. https://www.houstonchronicle.com/news/houston-texas/houston/article/Man-sentenced-for-luring-professor-into-online-4992027.php.

Schmidt, Michael S., William K. Rashbaum, Precioujs Fondren, and Adam Goldman. “People Tied to Project Veritas Scrutinized in Theft of Diary From Biden’s Daughter - The New York Times.” *New York Times* (Online). 5 November 2021. https://www.nytimes.com/2021/11/05/us/politics/project-veritas-investigation-ashley-biden-diary.html.

Schwartz, Brian. “Pro-Trump Lawyer Says His Plantations Were Go-to Spots for Those Aiming to Overturn the 2020 Election.” *CNBC*. 30 December 2021. https://www.cnbc.com/2021/12/30/pro-trump-lawyer-says-his-plantations-were-go-to-spots-for-election-conspiracy-theorists.html.

Schwarz, Kaylan C. “‘Gazing’ and ‘Performing’: Travel Photography and Online Self-Presentation.” *Tourist Studies* 21, no. 2 (2021): 260–77. doi: 10.1177/1468797620985789.

Scott, Eugene. “Trump’s Most Insulting — and Violent — Language Is Often Reserved for Immigrants.” *Washington Post*. 9 October 2019. https://www.washingtonpost.com/politics/2019/10/02/trumps-most-insulting-violent-language-is-often-reserved-immigrants/.

“Serbia Strong / Remove Kebab.” 2010. Know Your Meme. Accessed 9 August 2021. https://knowyourmeme.com/memes/serbia-strong-remove-kebab.

Smith, David. “South African Author ZP Dala Allegedly Coerced into Mental Hospital | South Africa | The Guardian.” 20 April 2015. https://www.theguardian

.com/world/2015/apr/12/south-african-muslim-author-z-p-dala-allegedly-coerced-mental-hospital.

Solove, Daniel. "Balkinization: Of Privacy and Poop: Norm Enforcement Via the Blogosphere." *Balkinization* (blog). 30 June 2005. https://balkin.blogspot.com/2005/06/of-privacy-and-poop-norm-enforcement.html.

Solove, Daniel J. "Introduction: When Poop Goes Primetime." In *The Future of Reputation*, 1–14. Gossip, Rumor, and Privacy on the Internet. Yale University Press, 2007.

———. "Shaming and the Digital Scarlet Letter." In *The Future of Reputation*, 76–102. Gossip, Rumor, and Privacy on the Internet. Yale University Press, 2007.

Sontag, Susan. *On Photography*. New York: Farrar, Straus and Giroux, 1977.

SPJ. "SPJ Code of Ethics - Society of Professional Journalists." 29 December 2021. https://www.spj.org/ethicscode.asp.

Stieber, Zachary. "Archdiocese Apologizes for Hasty Statement About Covington Students." *NTD News*. 24 January 2019. https://www.ntd.com/archdiocese-apologizes-for-hasty-statement-about-covington-students_280587.html.

Sydell, Laura. "Kyle Quinn Hid At A Friend's House After Being Misidentified On Twitter As A Racist." *NPR*. 17 August 2017, sec. Social Web. https://www.npr.org/sections/alltechconsidered/2017/08/17/543980653/kyle-quinn-hid-at-a-friend-s-house-after-being-misidentified-on-twitter-as-a-rac.

Tharoor, Ishaan. "Nobel Organization Decides to Condemn the Fatwa against Salman Rushdie, 27 Years Later - The Washington Post." 24 March 2016. https://www.washingtonpost.com/news/worldviews/wp/2016/03/24/nobel-organization-decides-to-condemn-the-fatwa-against-salman-rushdie-27-years-later/.

The Atlantic, dir. 2016. "Hail Trump!": Richard Spencer Speech Excerpts. https://www.youtube.com/watch?v=1o6-bi3jlxk.

Theimer, Sharon, and Peter Yost. "Did ACORN Get Too Big for Its Own Good?" 19 September 2009. https://www.nbcnews.com/id/wbna32925682.

Trefis Team. "Market Crashes Compared: -28% Coronavirus Crash Vs. 4 Historic Market Crashes." *Forbes*. 13 March 2020. https://www.forbes.com/sites/greatspeculations/2020/03/13/market-crashes-compared28-coronavirus-crash-vs-4-historic-market-crashes/.

Tripodi, Francesca Bolla. "ReOpen Demands as Public Health Threat: A Sociotechnical Framework for Understanding the Stickiness of Misinformation." *Computational and Mathematical Organization Theory* (August 10, 2021). doi: 10.1007/s10588-021-09339-8.

Trysnes, Irene, and Ronald Mayora Synnes. "The Role of Religion in Young Muslims' and Christians' Self-Presentation on Social Media." *YOUNG* 30, no. 3 (2022): 281–96. doi: 10.1177/11033088211063368.

Tufekci, Zeynep. "Can You See Me Now? Audience and Disclosure Regulation in Online Social Network Sites." *Bulletin of Science, Technology & Society* 28, no. 1 (2008): 20–36. doi: 10.1177/0270467607311484.

Ujifusa, Andrew. "Video of Boys Mocking Native American Vet, Unchecked by Adults, Sparks Uproar." *Education Week - Rules for Engagement*. 19 January

2019. http://blogs.edweek.org/edweek/rulesforengagement/2019/01/native-american-vietnam-veteran-abuse-teens-adults-uproar.html?cmp=SOC-SHR-FB.

Vaidhyanathan, S. *Antisocial Media: How Facebook Disconnects Us and Undermines Democracy*. New York: Oxford University Press, 2018.

Victor, Daniel. "Amateur Sleuths Aim to Identify Charlottesville Marchers, but Sometimes Misfire." *The New York Times*. 14 August 2017, sec. U.S. https://www.nytimes.com/2017/08/14/us/charlottesville-doxxing.html.

Waddell, T Franklin. "What Does the Crowd Think? How Online Comments and Popularity Metrics Affect News Credibility and Issue Importance." *New Media & Society* 20, no. 8 (2018): 3068–83. doi: 10.1177/1461444817742905.

Ward, Myah. "Appeals Court Rules New York Times Can Temporarily Keep Project Veritas Documents - POLITICO." 28 December 2021. https://www.politico.com/news/2021/12/28/appeals-court-says-new-york-times-can-temporarily-keep-project-veritas-documents-526229.

Washington Post Staff. "Project Veritas Response to DOJ." *Washington Post*. 22 November 2021. https://www.washingtonpost.com/context/project-veritas-response-to-doj/fb411800-fe8e-460e-8d76-269a357d4727/.

Weisman, J. *(((Semitism))): Being Jewish in America in the Age of Trump*. New York: St. Martin's Press, 2018.

Whalen, Jeanne. "Rupert Murdoch Remarks Secretly Recorded." *Wall Street Journal*, 4 July 2013. http://online.wsj.com/article/SB10001424127887323899704578585440176037904.html.

Williams, Apryl. "Black Memes Matter: #LivingWhileBlack with Becky and Karen." *Social Media + Society* 6, no. 4 (2020): 2056305120981047. doi: 10.1177/2056305120981047.

Williams, Kipling D. "Ostracism: The Kiss of Social Death." *Social and Personality Psychology Compass* 1, no. 1 (2007): 236–47. doi: 10.1111/j.1751-9004.2007.00004.x.

Witt, Lara. "I Was Doxxed By White Supremacists for Stepping Out of Line." *Wear Your Voice* (blog). 4 May 2021. https://www.wearyourvoicemag.com/i-was-doxxed-by-white-supremacists-for-stepping-out-of-line/.

Writers and Free Expression Team. "PEN Case Study: Salman Rushdie." *Writers and Free Expression* (blog). 23 April 2018. https://writersandfreeexpression.com/2018/04/23/pen-case-study-salman-rushdie/.

Wulfson, Joseph A. "College Professor Fired For Posting Online That Otto Warmbier 'Got What He Deserved.'" *Mediaite* (blog). 26 June 2017. https://www.mediaite.com/online/college-professor-fired-for-posting-online-that-otto-warmbier-got-what-he-deserved/.

Index

About the Author

Jessica Emami, PhD, is an adjunct professor of Sociology at American University in Washington, DC. Her areas of expertise include digital sociology, antisemitism, and globalization. A lifelong teacher and researcher, Jessica has presented on the intersection of technology and society for the American Sociological Association, Eastern Sociological Society, Southern Sociological Society, and other professional groups. She lives in the Washington, DC, metropolitan area with her spouse.

www.ingramcontent.com/pod-product-compliance
Ingram Content Group UK Ltd.
Pitfield, Milton Keynes, MK11 3LW, UK
UKHW041452071026
15587UKWH00010B/919

9 781793 629647